THE LANGUAGE OF LITERATURE

by

DAVID CLARKE

Headmaster, Sandbach High School, Cheshire

Designed by **Roger Sadler**

HOLMES McDOUGALL
EDINBURGH

Printed and published by
Holmes McDougall Ltd.,
Allander House,
137-141 Leith Walk,
Edinburgh EH6 8NS.

Set in Plantin, 10 on 12 pt.

ISBN: 7157 1870-3

CONTENTS

INTRODUCTION

ACKNOWLEDGMENTS

The author and publishers are grateful for the help and co-operation of the Headmaster, staff and pupils of Alsager Comprehensive School, Cheshire, in the preparation of Section C of this book and to the following for permission to reproduce copyright material in this book:

Basil Blackwell & Mott Ltd for Humbert Wolfe, *The Grey Squirrel*, p. 8; William Heinemann Ltd, Laurence Pollinger Ltd and the Estate of the late Mrs Frieda Lawrence Ravagli for D. H. Lawrence, *Fish* p. 9 from his *Collected Poems*, 'Nottingham and the Mining Countryside' from *Phoenix, Sons and Lovers*, 'Odour of Chrysanthemums' from his *Collected Stories*; Faber and Faber Ltd for Robert Lowell, *For the Union Dead*, p. 11, and 'Waking Early Sunday Morning', p. 13 from *Near the Ocean*, Seamus Heaney, 'Trout' from *Death of a Naturalist*, Ted Hughes, 'Her Husband' from *Wodwo*, 'Wind', p. 26 from *The Hawk in the Rain*, 'To Paint a Water Lily', *from Lupercal*, extract from *Poetry in the Making*, 'The Thought Fox' from *The Hawk in the Rain*, 'Thistles' from *Wodwo*, W. H. Auden, 'Night Mail' and 'The Unknown Citizen' from his *Collected Shorter Poems*, Philip Larkin, 'Days', 'An Arundel Tomb', 'Whitsun Weddings', 'Afternoons', from *The Whitsun Weddings*, Louis MacNeice, 'Pet Shop', from his *Collected Poems*, Siegfried Sassoon, *Memoirs of an Infantry Officer*; Mrs Myfanwy Thomas and Faber & Faber Ltd for Edward Thomas, *Aspens*; Carcanet Press Ltd for Edwin Morgan, 'For Bonfires' p. 12, 'Death in Duke Street' p. 13, 'The Post Office Tower', 'Interferences' p. 53, 'A Glasgow Sonnet' from *From Glasgow to Saturn, The Loch Ness Monster's Song*; London Magazine 1967 for Edwin Morgan, *The Computer's First Christmas Card*; J. M. Dent & Sons Ltd and the Trustees for the late Dylan Thomas for *Under Milk Wood*, 'Poem in October' from his *Collected Poems*, 'Holiday Memory' from *Quite Early One Morning*; Oxford University Press for Charles Tomlinson, 'Winter-Piece' from *A Peopled Landscape*, Tony Connor, 'In Oak Terrace' and 'Entering the City' from *Lodgers*; Curtis Brown Ltd and the Estate of John Steinbeck for *The Pearl*; John Junor for 'Current Events', p. 26, from the *Sunday Express*; John Murray (Publishers) Ltd for John Betjeman, 'In Westminster Abbey', 'St Katherine Chiselhampton', 'The Village Inn' from his *Collected Poems*; Gerald Duckworth & Co Ltd and A. D. Peters & Co Ltd for Hilaire Belloc, *Tarantella*; Ebury Press © The National Magazine Co Ltd 1972 for part of recipe 'Veal in Sherry Sauce' from *Good Housekeeping Home Freezer Cook Book*; George Allen & Unwin (Publishers) Ltd for J. R. R. Tolkien, *Silmarillion*; Jonathan Cape Ltd and the Executors of the Ernest Hemingway Estate for 'In Our Time' from *The First Forty-nine Stories*; NATO Review for James Huntley, *The Global Significance of the Evolving Atlantic-Pacific System*; HMSO for Winston Churchill, *Speech to Parliament* quoted in Hansard; Martin Secker & Warburg, Arthur Miller, 'Death of a Salesman', © 1949 by Arthur Miller from his *Collected Plays*; Eyre Methuen Ltd for Harold Pinter, 'Last to Go' from *A Slight Ache and Other Plays*; Chatto and Windus Ltd and Heron Press (USA) for Jon Silkin, *Death of a Son*; Mrs Sonia Brownell Orwell and Martin Secker & Warburg Ltd for George Orwell, *Down and Out in Paris and London* and *Animal Farm*; John Calder (Publishers) Ltd for Samuel Beckett, 'Still' from *For to End Yet Again*; Michael Joseph Ltd for Barry Hines, *A Kestrel for a Knave*; Andre Deutsch for John Updike, *The Centaur* and V. S. Naipaul, *Mr Stone and the Knights Companion*; John Carey for *Burning Children*; London Management Ltd for Peter Shaffer, *Five Finger Exercise*; Constable & Co Ltd for Leon Garfield, *Mr Corbett's Ghost*; *Saturday Review* for James L. Rosenberg, *The Wasps' Nest*; William Heinemann Ltd for Richard Church, *Over the Bridge*; William Heinemann Ltd and A. D. Peters & Co Ltd for John Whiting, *The Devils*; Vernon Scannell for *First Child*; James Kirkup for *Rugby League Game*; Margaret Stanley-Wrench for *Coalmine*; Yale University Press for Robert Horan, *Little City*.

The author and publishers have made every effort to trace the copyright of the material used in this book and in any case where they have been unsuccessful apologise for any accidental infringement of copyright.

INTRODUCTION

This book has developed from the author's experience as a teacher and as a chief examiner over many years. Its frankly utilitarian approach to examinations in English Literature should not be allowed to obscure its deeper purposes. Any syllabus leading to an external examination in English Literature will have as one of its main aims the intention of encouraging young people to respond with judgement and sensitivity, and in some depth, to prose and poetry of quality. This is a worthy aim and one with which this book is entirely in sympathy.

It is sad to see how seldom this aim is fully achieved in the examination room. To judge from many thousands of scripts marked by the author at CSE, 16+, 'O' and 'A' level, this skill of responding with judgement and sensitivity is a skill which has continued to elude many pupils by the time they leave school.

There are many reasons for this. One main reason is that many examination candidates are unaware of, or have not grasped, the appropriate technical terms they need to know, and so often don't know how to tackle the questions in an informed way. They are uncertain about methods and approaches. A basic aim of this book is to help to put right these deficiencies.

Current theories about language across the curriculum have focused attention on the need for all teachers to increase their understanding and awareness of their own and of others' use and handling of language. It has been clearly demonstrated that language plays a central role in the generating of knowledge and that each subject has its own specialist terminology. In English Literature just as much as in the Sciences or in practical subjects such as Home Economics or Technical Studies there are certain specialist terms which have to be understood before a pupil can make progress. There are particular concepts and methods of approach which have to be mastered and which differ from subject to subject. For success to be achieved the teacher and pupil (and examiner) must talk the same language. Just as a pupil needs to understand *basic shape, raising agent, force, cottage industry* in other areas of the curriculum, so in English Literature he needs to understand and be able to talk and write intelligently about *images, diction, effectiveness* and the like. He needs to be shown what to look for in a piece of writing and how to comment in an informed way on what he finds there. He must be taught how to respond. He must be taught the language of literature.

The purpose of this book, then, is to aid the teaching processes by which a pupil becomes aware of the richness and variety of English Literature. The book provides him with explanations, models and examples, and, in so doing, offers him practical help towards success at the end of an examination course.

The book is in four sections. The first section introduces the reader to a variety of literary terms: imagery, diction, contrasts, character, rhythm, and the like. Practical exercises are included where appropriate.

The second section contains poems by four poets, chosen because their work is often set at CSE and GCE 'O' level and also because they offer a certain amount of difficulty for young people. Where appropriate, each poem is followed by a prose summary of each verse of the poem, so that something of the meaning and structure of the poem is made clear, and this summary is followed by a detailed appreciation of the poem.

Section C consists of passages and questions of the kind set in external examinations together with answers of high quality written by pupils under examination conditions. These answers have been marked in detail, so that the reader has a clear idea what the examiner is looking for and what sort of comment and approach will earn reward. At the end of the answers there are further notes for guidance: suggestions, for example, as to where an answer could have been improved, or why a particular point is not acceptable.

The last section of the book (Section D) consists of twenty exercises (ten prose passages and ten poems) with questions of the type normally found in 'O' level and CSE examinations. The work here is based entirely on what has gone before in Sections A, B and C, the questions being of the literary comprehension and appreciation type. As such they are by no means confined to those who study for English Literature papers. They may well be relevant to pupils who are taking English Language at 'O' level.

The book is generally intended to serve pupils from the end of the fourth year and upwards in secondary schools. It is primarily intended for those taking 'O' level, CSE or 16+ examinations, but it will also be found helpful to those pupils who are studying English in their first year in the sixth form or in colleges of further education.

This book does not try to cover everything and herein, the author hopes, lies its strength as a teaching tool in the classroom. If the pupils, guided carefully by their teacher, can grasp the concepts and approaches outlined in these pages, they will establish for themselves the strong foundations upon which further courses of advanced study can be built. Especially in Sections A, B and C is this guidance from and discussion with the teacher necessary. Much of the material in these sections is meant to be read and worked through together. The author also hopes that the book will be of service to those teachers whose specialism is not English but who teach English Literature as part of their timetable.

David Clarke

TECHNICAL TERMS — A

INTRODUCTION

Every subject that you study in school has its own language, its own special words that you need to master and understand if you are to make progress in that subject.

The following words are just a few examples. Can you identify the subject areas where they are most likely to be used?

plankton	whisk the ingredients	quantum theory
eternity	milles	milling machine
footwork	perspective	chapter

English Literature is no exception. It has its own special language with which you need to become familiar if you are to learn how to talk about the language in which good literature is written.

This section of the book is devoted, therefore, to *technical terms* in order to help you with the special words and concepts used in responding to English Literature. In this section you will find information you will need to know when working through Sections B and C and when answering the questions on the prose passages and poems in Section D.

Make sure you understand these *technical terms* before you deal with the later sections of the book, and then use Section A when necessary as a short handbook of guidance or reference.

IMAGES

I

When you look in a mirror, you see an *image*. You see a likeness of yourself. When you use a camera and take a picture of Aunt Martha in a flowered hat, the photograph you develop is an *image* of her. If you look at the photograph twenty years later, you will see an *image* of what Aunt Martha used to look like. ("Poor soul, she's dead now!")

You might ask a famous painter to paint your portrait in oils. The picture he paints is an *image* of you. It may not be exactly like you. He may get your nose bent round a bit the wrong way, or he may not capture in quite the way you wanted the truly ravishing nature of your blood-red eyes. He may give you a figure the size of a front row forward, when you have always thought of yourself as slim, or at most modestly ample, but certainly not built like a tank. But if your friends say, "What a good likeness of Tom or Josephine," the unpleasant truth may dawn on you that their *image* of you, their mental picture of what you are like, is not quite the same as your own. And the artist, remember, is world famous. He has painted you as he sees you. He has put on to canvas his *image* of you. Perhaps he has tried to convey in his picture not only your physical likeness but also something of your inner character: how greedy you are, for example.

The same with words. Instead of painting you in oils, someone may prefer to paint you in words. If you really are greedy and have no table manners at all, you may one day find, at your table in the exclusive restaurant where you often dine, written on a small white card, the terse message

YOU'RE A PIG.

The writer of that unfriendly note (I promised not to reveal his identity since he is a friend of yours) is using an *image* when he writes

YOU'RE A PIG.

You are not a pig, of course, even though your table manners are dreadful. What the writer means is that you eat like a pig. You are like a pig in this one respect. There is no suggestion in this statement that physically you actually look like a pig.

There could be. There would be, if the writer went on to say

FURTHERMORE, I DON'T LIKE YOUR SNOUT
OR YOUR LITTLE PIGGY EYES
AND PINK SKIN.

The comparison is now physical. Not only are you greedy like a pig you actually look like one. A snout, piggy eyes, and a pink skin are the similar physical characteristics you share with the pig. And finally, if the writer concludes with the command

GET BACK TO YOUR STY!

you can be sure he is not impressed by your home or the other members of your family.

PIG—SNOUT—LITTLE PIGGY EYES—STY are all *images*. They are all making comparisons. They all suggest that you are like a pig.

So, an *image* is a likeness. A comparison. A picture. It may be yourself in the mirror, or a photograph, or a painting, or a vivid description in words.

Let us concentrate on *images in words*.

II
Look at these examples:

1. West Ham's goalkeeper is *as nimble as a cat*.

2. *Like a small grey
    coffee-pot,*
    sits the squirrel.

3. John runs *like a hare*.

Each of these examples contains an image (the words in italics). When an image contains the word *like* or *as*, it is easy to recognise. You probably know that this type of image is called a *simile*. The word *like* or *as* provides the clue: it shows that something is similar to something else in one particular respect.

In the first example West Ham's goalkeeper is compared with a cat. That doesn't mean that he actually looks like a cat any more than you looked like a pig a few minutes ago. The one point of the comparison is that the goalkeeper is as quick in movement, as agile, as a cat.

The point of comparison in the second example is easy to identify. Here the shape of the squirrel as it sits on its haunches is compared with the shape of a coffee-pot, with the squirrel's paws and bushy tail looking like the coffee-pot's spout and handle.

The third image is also easy. The comparison here is between John's speed of running and the speed of a hare. Speed is the one appropriate quality which John shares with a hare, and you would do violence to the image, and reduce it to absurdity, if you tried to make the point of comparison the idea that they both moved in the same way!

FOR DISCUSSION

For each of the following explain clearly what two things are being compared and say in what particular respect they are being compared. In the first three questions the words which are images have been put in italics to help you. In the rest you first have to find the image for yourself.

1. Robert's skin is *like sandpaper*.

2. I saw, dimly,
   Once a big pike rush,
   And small fish fly *like splinters*.

3. *Like as the waves make towards the pebbled shore,*
   So do our minutes hasten to their end;
   Each changing place with that which goes before,
   In sequent toil all forwards do contend.

4. The coarse grass bristled in the wind like a living pelt.

5. Jane has teeth like a horse.

6. It is a beauteous evening, calm and free;
   The holy time is quiet as a nun
   Breathless with adoration.

7. Like a man with a scythe Time cuts us down.

8. Then the whining school-boy, with his satchel
   And shining morning face, creeping like snail
   Unwillingly to school.

III

Not all images contain the word *like* or *as* and when an image does not contain these words it is more difficult to identify. For example, we could have written

John *hared* off down the road.

Robert has *sandpaper* skin.

Time *scythes* us down.

Each word in italics is still an image and the point of comparison remains exactly the same, but the image is more difficult to find because it is not so clearly sign-posted. Study this example:

With a bonfire throat,
Legs of twig,
A dark brown coat,
The inspector robin
Comes where I dig.

There are three images here: *bonfire, of twig, inspector*. The hidden comparison in each image is soon revealed by turning the words into similes:

With a throat *like a bonfire*

With legs *like twigs*

The robin *like an inspector*

Once you have done this, the comparison in each image becomes clear:

The redness of the robin's throat is compared with the red blaze of a bonfire.

The robin's legs are compared with twigs in their thinness and/or brittleness.

The robin watching the man dig is compared with someone who inspects or supervises someone else working. It is as if the robin were actually assessing the work being done.

Images which don't use *like* or *as* are often called *metaphors*.

The word pictures in the poem (*bonfire, of twig, inspector*) and *hared, sandpaper,* and *scythes* are all images. They are all metaphors.

A *metaphor* simply means a description of one thing in terms of something else.

Very large numbers of words in English can be used as images/metaphors and indeed are used in this way both by writers and by people generally in their ordinary, everyday speech.

For example, you might write:

> The ship cuts its way through the sea as a plough cuts its way through the earth.

But it is simpler and quicker to write:

> The ship ploughed through the sea.

ploughed is an image, a metaphor. So are these, all taken from everyday speech and all familiar to you:

> There's not *a shadow of doubt* about it.

> He has a heart *of stone*.

> They spoke some *heated words*.

Here is another example:

> One morning last March
> I pressed against the new barbed and galvanized
> fence on the Boston Common. Behind their cage,
> yellow dinosaur steamshovels were grunting
> as they cropped up tons of mush and grass
> to gouge their underworld garage.

The steamshovels are like dinosaurs feeding on the mush and grass. They resemble dinosaurs in their shape, with their elongated bodies and the large scoops at the top being like gigantic mouths chewing food. But notice how the idea of the *dinosaur* image is extended to other things. The steamshovels are *grunting* (like animals) and the poet thinks of the fence, which is constructed to keep people off the building site, as a *cage*, behind which the dinosaurs are free to roam and eat. He himself looks on at them as if he were a visitor at a zoo.

To sum up, then. An image is a word picture. It may be a simile, a straightforward comparison:

> Death comes *like a thief in the night*.

Or it may be a metaphor, a hidden comparison, which describes one thing in terms of something else:

> Death *robbed* the nation of its most promising young composer and pianist.

In each case the meaning is conveyed to us through a word picture. The comparison conjures up the idea in our minds by giving us a mental picture of Death as a robber.

IV   FOR DISCUSSION

1.   Identify the metaphors in the following everyday expressions:

> A faint ray of hope shone through the gloom.
> She collapsed in a flood of tears.
> He has no spark of intelligence.

2.   "Images usually try to make abstract ideas concrete." In discussion with your teacher make sure you understand the terms *abstract* and *concrete* as they are used in this sentence.

3.   Discuss with your teacher the difference between *literal truth* and *metaphorical truth*.

4.   How is war like (i) a storm, (ii) a plague, (iii) a hero's dream, (iv) a scar on the face of the earth, (v) music?

5.   For each of the following put the words in column (a) with the most suitable words in column (b) so that an image is formed. Then explain the point of the comparison.

(a)		(b)
Rain	is	the hammer of God
Anger	is	a many-headed beast
Peace	is	a firework
Poverty	is	a journey
A traitor	is	a rose
Life	is	a prison
Thunder	is	sadness
A crowd	is	a snake

6.   What alternative readings can you form from combining columns (a) and (b) in Question 5 above? What combinations are clearly unacceptable?

7.   Make up your own images, using each of the following words:

> *river   star   road   stinging   fire*

V   WRITTEN WORK

1.   The following passages contain a number of images (shown in italics). For each image explain clearly what two things are being compared and say in what particular respect they are being compared.

> (a)   In a galvanized bucket
>   the letters burn. They roar and twist
>   and the leaves curl back one by one.
>   *They put out claws and scrape the iron*
>   *like a living thing,*
>   *but the scrabbling to be free soon subsides.*

(b) No mockeries now for them; no prayers nor bells,
Nor any voice of mourning save the choirs,
The shrill, demented *choirs* of wailing shells;
And bugles calling for them from sad shires.

(c) My soul *is an enchanted boat*,
Which, *like a sleeping swan*, doth *float*
Upon *the silver waves* of thy sweet singing.

(d) No weekends for the gods now. Wars
flicker, *earth licks its open sores*,
fresh breakage, fresh promotions, chance
assassinations, no advance.
Only man thinning out his kind
sounds through the Sabbath noon, the blind
swipe of *the pruner and his knife*
busy about the tree of life.

(e) He seems not to be in pain,
he is speaking slowly and quietly
but he does not look at any of them,
his eyes are fixed on the sky,
already *he is moving out*
beyond everything belonging.
As if he still belonged
they hold him very tight.
Only *the hungry ambulance*
howls for him through the *staring* squares.

2.   Study this paragraph:

A stout man with a pink face wears dingy white flannel trousers, a blue
coat with a pink handkerchief showing, and a straw hat much too
small for him, perched at the back of his head. He plays the guitar. A
little chap in white canvas shoes, his face hidden under a felt hat like a
broken wing, breathes into a flute; and a tall thin fellow, with bursting 5
over-ripe boots, draws ribbons—long, twisted, streaming ribbons—
of tune out of a fiddle. They stand, unsmiling, but not serious, in the
broad sunlight opposite the fruit-shop; the pink spider of a hand beats
the guitar, the little squat hand, with a brass-and-turquoise ring,
forces the reluctant flute, and the fiddler's arm tries to saw the fiddle 10
in two.

What do the images in the above paragraph suggest are the writer's feelings about the
musicians and their performance?

3.   Identify and explain *three* images in the following extract, which is taken from a
poem describing the view from the Post Office Tower, London.

On a roof southward, broken concrete
between two chimneys blossoms
in a line of washing, an old man
on a hard chair, his hands in his lap,
stares at nothing—linen flowers   5
tugging to be free. And like some fine insect
poised on a blackened outcrop of stone
a young man mends an aerial far down the central haze,
straddles a fire-escape in ice-blue jeans
and striped shirt, arms bare to the shoulder and his hair   10
is blown across his arms
as he moves the metal arms
into the path of their messages.
—And all that grace to dwindle to
a faded dressing-gown, a kitchen chair in the sun.   15

VI

The following poem is rather remarkable for its *imagery*. (When a writer uses a lot of images, we speak of his use of *imagery*. This simply means his collection of images, the images he has collected together in one place. They may be a collection of completely different images, or they may be very similar in idea.) Most of the images, but not all, in this poem by Seamus Heaney illustrate the same idea: that of a trout described in military images. Read the poem and discuss it with your teacher.

Trout

Hangs, a fat gun-barrel,
deep under arched bridges
or slips like butter down
the throat of the river.

From depths smooth-skinned as plums   5
his muzzle gets bull's eye;
picks off grass-seed and moths
that vanish, torpedoed.

Where water unravels
over gravel-beds he   10
is fired from the shadows
white belly reporting

flat; darts like a tracer-
bullet back between stones
and is never burnt out.   15
A volley of cold blood

ramrodding the current.

VII

Now that you have some idea of what an image is, it is as well to ask yourself a few basic questions. Why do writers use images? Why bother to write in this way? Why write at all?

Let us take the last question first. The answer is quite simple. All writing (and reading) is a main way of sharing experience, just as talking (and listening) is another way. If you then ask, "Well, why bother to share experience?" the answer, again, is straight-forward. We all do it all the time. It is in our nature as human beings to communicate with each other. We tell each other things we think are of interest and value. Most of the time we do it through talk rather than through writing. We talk about music, or a film we have seen, or a book we have read, or about some recent event that has captured the news headlines. We talk about politics, or the weather, or the price of shoes, or whether Manchester United will win on Saturday, or our hopes for the future, or our jobs, or our relatives, or neighbours, or friends, or what happened at school. When a close friend goes away for some time, we might talk to him on the telephone. Failing that, we will write him a letter. It will tell him something.

The writer does the same thing. He puts words on paper because he wants to tell you something. He wants to share his knowledge and experience with you, and he thinks it is important enough to take the trouble to write it down on paper. He may be a scientist, who has worked out a new theory which needs to be explained. In this case the article he writes will both *inform and instruct* you. Or he may be a motor engineer or a surveyor, *advising* you in a report on the car or house you are thinking of buying. A politician will try to *persuade* you to his point of view. The novelist will try to *entertain* you by telling you a story. And it is the creative writer (the novelist, the playwright, the poet) who most often uses images.

Why?

Notice that the words *image* and *imagery* are connected with the word *imagination*.

By using images the writer tries to tell you *what it was like*.

In telling you *what it was like* the writer uses images which will suggest things to you and spark off your imagination. He tries to make real to you his experience by bringing into play your senses—of sight, sound, taste, smell and touch. His experience may deal with a whole range of things, from the trivial to lasting and important things like the purpose of life, love, death and the question of an after-life. Whatever his subject, in sharing his experience with us, in telling us *what it was like*, the good writer often enriches our own experience by making us aware of ideas and points of view which we weren't aware of before. The poem, *Trout*, for example, in its unusual description of the fish, is an instance of this.

VIII
The poems and passages which follow all describe different areas of experience and use different images to make the experience real to you. Discuss them with your teacher.

Her Husband

Comes home dull with coal-dust deliberately
To grime the sink and foul towels and let her
Learn with scrubbing brush and scrubbing board
The stubborn character of money.

And let her learn through what kind of dust   5
He has earned his thirst and the right to quench it
And what sweat he has exchanged for his money
And the blood-weight of money. He'll humble her

With new light on her obligations.
The fried, woody chips, kept warm two hours in the oven,   10
Are only part of her answer.
Hearing the rest, he slams them to the fire back

And is away round the house-end singing
'Come back to Sorrento' in a voice
Of resounding corrugated iron.   15
Her back has bunched into a hump as an insult.

For they will have their rights.
Their jurors are to be assembled
From the little crumbs of soot. Their brief
Goes straight up to heaven and nothing more is heard of it.   20

Ted Hughes

It is spring, moonless night in the small town, starless and bible-black,
the cobblestreets silent and the hunched, courters'-and-rabbits' wood
limping invisible down to the sloeblack, slow, black, crowblack,
fishingboat-bobbing sea. The houses are blind as moles (though moles
see fine tonight in the snouting, velvet dingles) or blind as Captain Cat 5
there in the muffled middle by the pump and the town clock, the
shops in mourning, the Welfare Hall in widows' weeds. And all the
people of the lulled and dumbfound town are sleeping now.

Dylan Thomas (from **Under Milk Wood***)*

Aspens

All day and night, save winter, every weather,
Above the inn, the smithy, and the shop,
The aspens at the cross-roads talk together
Of rain, until their last leaves fall from the top.

Out of the blacksmith's cavern comes the ringing   5
Of hammer, shoe, and anvil; out of the inn
The clink, the hum, the roar, the random singing—
The sounds that for these fifty years have been.

The whisper of the aspens is not drowned,
And over lightless pane and footless road,   10
Empty as sky, with every other sound
Not ceasing, calls their ghosts from their abode,

A silent smithy, a silent inn, nor fails
In the bare moonlight or the thick-furred gloom,
In tempest or the night of nightingales,   15
To turn the cross-roads to a ghostly room.

And it would be the same were no house near.
Over all sorts of weather, men, and times,
Aspens must shake their leaves and men may hear
But need not listen, more than to my rhymes.   20

Whatever wind blows, while they and I have leaves
We cannot other than an aspen be
That ceaselessly, unreasonably grieves,
Or so men think who like a different tree.

Edward Thomas

London

I wander thro' each charter'd street,
Near where the charter'd Thames does flow
And mark in every face I meet
Marks of weakness, marks of woe.

In every cry of every Man,   5
In every Infants cry of fear,
In every voice; in every ban,
The mind-forg'd manacles I hear

How the Chimney-sweepers cry
Every blackning Church appalls,   10
And the hapless Soldiers sigh
Runs in blood down Palace walls

But most thro' midnight streets I hear
How the youthful Harlots curse
Blasts the new-born Infants tear   15
And blights with plagues the Marriage hearse.

William Blake

Rugby League Game

Sport is absurd, and sad.
Those grown men, just look,
In those dreary long blue shorts,
Those ringed stockings, Edwardian,
Balding pates, and huge   5
Fat knees that ought to be heroes'.

Grappling, hooking, gallantly tackling—
Is all this courage really necessary?—
Taking their good clean fun
So solemnly, they run each other down   10
With earnest keenness, for the honour of
Virility, the cap, the county side.

Like great boys they roll each other
In the mud of public Saturdays,
Groping their blind way back   15
To noble youth, away from the bank,
The wife, the pram, the spin drier,
Back to the Spartan freedom of the field.

Back, back to the days when boys
Were men, still hopeful, and untamed.   20
That was then: a gay
And golden age ago.
Now, in vain, domesticated,
Men try to be boys again.

James Kirkup

It was a town of red brick, or of brick that would have been red if the
smoke and ashes had allowed it; but as matters stood it was a town of
unnatural red and black like the painted face of a savage. It was a town
of machinery and tall chimneys, out of which interminable serpents of
smoke trailed themselves for ever and ever, and never got uncoiled. It 5
had a black canal in it, and a river that ran purple with ill-smelling dye,
and vast piles of buildings full of windows where there was a rattling
and a trembling all day long, and where the piston of the steam-engine
worked monotonously up and down like the head of an elephant in a
state of melancholy madness.   10

Charles Dickens (from **Hard Times***)*

During Wind and Rain

They sing their dearest songs—
He, she, all of them—yea,
Treble and tenor and bass,
   And one to play;
With the candles mooning each face . . .   5
   Ah, no; the years O!
How the sick leaves reel down in throngs!

They clear the creeping moss—
Elders and juniors—aye,
Making the pathways neat   10
   And the garden gay;
And they build a shady seat . . .

Ah, no; the years, the years;
See, the white storm-birds wing across.

They are blithely breakfasting all—   15
Men and maidens—yea,
Under the summer tree,
    With a glimpse of the bay,
While pet fowl come to the knee . . .
    Ah, no; the years O!   20
And the rotten rose is ript from the wall.

They change to a high new house,
He, she, all of them—aye,
Clocks and carpets and chairs
    On the lawn all day,   25
And brightest things that are theirs . . . ·
    Ah, no; the years, the years;
Down their carved names the rain-drop ploughs.

                                                    Thomas Hardy

Winter-Piece

You wake, all windows blind—embattled sprays
grained on the mediaeval glass.
Gates snap like gunshot
as you handle them. Five-barred fragility
sets flying fifteen rooks who go together   5
silently ravenous above this winter-piece
that will not feed them. They alight
beyond, scavenging, missing everything
but the bladed atmosphere, the white resistance.
Ruts with iron flanges track   10
through a hard decay
where you discern once more
oak-leaf by hawthorn, for the frost
rewhets their edges. In a perfect web
blanched along each spoke   15
and circle of its woven wheel,
the spider hangs, grasp unbroken
and death-masked in cold. Returning
you see the house glint-out behind
its holed and ragged glaze,   20
frost-fronds all streaming.

                                                Charles Tomlinson

IX

Let us end our discussions on images with two dictionary definitions:

IMAGE   A likeness, a symbol; a mental representation; a vivid description; a simile,
          metaphor, or figure of speech

IMAGERY   The use of images collectively; figurative illustration

DICTION: The Writer's Choice of Words

I

To study a writer's diction is to study his choice of words, and in studying his choice of words you need to consider two questions:

1)   Why has the writer chosen these words on this occasion?

and/or .

2)   What is the effect of these words, either separately or how they work together?

The first question is directed at discovering the writer's intention, the second at analysing what the reader's response ought to be to the written words. In practice the questions are closely interrelated and it is not always possible to separate them completely. Often a writer chooses certain words with the intention of getting you, the reader, to respond in a particular way, so that the writer's intention and the reader's response amount to the same thing. In other words you get the same answer when you ask yourself each of the above questions.

II

Let us take an example which will show just how important the choice of a single word can be. It is the opening sentence of a newspaper report, written a few years ago:

Archbishop Makarios was warned to-day to stay away from Cyprus.

This sentence tells us one fact, easy to understand. For some reason (which the report goes on later to make clear) the Archbishop is not welcome in Cyprus. The same fact would be communicated to us if the sentence read:

Archbishop Makarios was advised to-day to stay away from Cyprus.

or

Archbishop Makarios was asked to-day to stay away from Cyprus.

But there is a slight difference in the meaning of each sentence, brought about by the changing of a single word. The first sentence is hostile: *warned* is a threatening word. It is used in sentences like "I'm warning you", "Be warned", "This is your last warning!" and it suggests that something nasty and unpleasant will happen if you don't heed the warning. Similarly, in this report the word is used in an aggressive way. The writer has chosen this particular word to indicate the strength of feeling against the Archbishop on the part of his enemies.

Advised, if used, would alter the meaning of the report. In the idea of advising there is the suggestion that the advice is given for the benefit of the Archbishop, for his own good. In other words *advised* is a positive word, as if the adviser is on the same side as the Archbishop. It is a helpful word. It gives good counsel and is not threatening in any way.

Asked is more vague. In using this word it may be implied that the Archbishop would be granting someone a favour by staying away from Cyprus, but the word *asked* is nothing like as strong as *warned* and is neutral compared with *advised*. It makes a request, but does not force the issue.

III

The example we have just considered deals with the choice of a single word, but more often in English Literature you will find the writer's careful choice of words, his *diction*, is sustained at greater length and for deliberate purposes. Here are two very different examples:

> There was a steaming mist in all the hollows, and it had roamed in its
> forlornness up the hill, like an evil spirit, seeking rest and finding
> none. A clammy and intensely cold mist, it made its slow way through
> the air in ripples that visibly followed and overspread one another, as
> the waves of an unwholesome sea might do. It was dense enough to   5
> shut out everything from the light of the coach-lamps but these its own
> workings, and a few yards of road; and the reek of the labouring horses
> steamed into it, as if they had made it all.

> The world is charged with the grandeur of God.
> It will flame out, like shining from shook foil;
> It gathers to a greatness, like the ooze of oil
> Crushed. Why do men then now not reck his rod?
> Generations have trod, have trod, have trod;   5
> And all is seared with trade; bleared, smeared with toil;
> And wears man's smudge, and shares man's smell: the soil
> Is bare now, nor can foot feel, being shod.

> And for all this, nature is never spent;
> There lives the dearest freshness deep down things;   10
> And though the last lights off the black West went
> Oh, morning, at the brown brink eastward, springs—
> Because the Holy Ghost over the bent
> World broods with warm breast and with ah! bright wings.

The second example is a poem called *God's Grandeur* by Gerard Manley Hopkins. It is easy to see at a glance that it uses language in totally different ways from the first example, but it is harder to say what are these ways.

Look again at the first passage. (It is from *A Tale of Two Cities* by Charles Dickens.) *Why has Dickens chosen these words on this occasion?* The answer is simple. He wants to describe the unpleasant nature of a particular mist.

What, then, is the effect of these words? This question is not so easy to answer, but we do get a sense of the mist's movement in a word like *steaming*, which suggests its turbulent, boiling motion, and in words like *roamed*, suggesting restlessness, and *made its slow way . . . in ripples*, suggesting a creeping effect. We are shown the chilling effect of the mist (it is *clammy and intensely cold*) and its power to isolate is given in the words *dense enough to shut out everything*. Throughout the paragraph Dickens dwells on the mist's unhealthy, almost supernatural qualities: *forlornness, like an evil spirit, unwholesome*. The passage ends with the imaginative suggestion that the mist has all come from the sweating horses.

God's Grandeur uses language in an original and dramatic way. *Why has the poet chosen these words to write a poem like this?* Well, the answer is bound up with the poet's subject matter and his attitude towards it. Look at what the words are actually saying. The poem is about the grandeur, or greatness, of God. It tells us that men do not have any regard for God's authority; but, despite man's despoiling of the world, nature is eternal and fresh and is forever renewed, because it is in God's care. Hopkins wants us to know this and to share his belief that God's love is all-embracing.

What, then, is the effect of these words? To begin with, in words such as *charged, flame out,* and *shining from shook foil,* Hopkins vividly conveys the pent-up force, the surging power and dazzling brightness of God's greatness and majesty. In contrast, the repetition of *have trod* in line 5 shows that man limits himself to an existence which is monotonously always the same, consisting merely of ordinary *trade* and *toil*. Man's pollution of the world is given by *seared, bleared, smeared*. His *smudge* defiles everything, and he has lost contact with nature: *nor can foot feel, being shod.*

Even so, nature is never completely worn out or destroyed (*spent*). Though *the soil/Is bare*, suggesting winter, at the heart of things is a pure and precious originality (*dearest freshness*) which God creates and renews. At the very moment night falls (*the black West*) the sun rises in the east and darkness gives way to light. Morning *springs*: the word suggests energy and growth. *Oh* and *ah*! are quiet exclamations which reveal the poet's reverence for the grandeur of God. The image of a dove, or an angel, in the last line of the sonnet conveys peace and security (*broods with warm breast*) and the beauty (*bright wings*) of the Holy Ghost.

Much could be said about the poet's masterly control of rhythm and rhyme, but the total effect of the words, the *diction*, is to convince us of the wonder and optimism of Hopkins's religious experience.

IV

Let us take another example, this time from *The Winter's Tale* by William Shakespeare. Leontes, the King of Sicilia, wrongly accuses Hermione, his wife, of having an adulterous relationship with Polixenes, the King of Bohemia. In his jealous fury he casts out his new-born daughter, believing the child not to be his, and tries to kill Polixenes, but Polixenes escapes. Hermione dies of grief. Later Leontes discovers his error and spends many years in deep repentance, trying to atone for his sins. Eventually he is visited by the son of Polixenes in the company of the young and beautiful girl he intends to marry. Leontes is overjoyed at meeting them and speaks the following lines:

> The blessed gods
> Purge all infection from our air, whilst you
> Do climate here! You have a holy father,
> A graceful gentleman; against whose person
> (So sacred as it is) I have done sin,   5
> For which, the heavens (taking angry note)
> Have left me issueless: and your father's blest
> (As he from heaven merits it) with you,
> Worthy his goodness. What might I have been,
> Might I a son and daughter now have look'd on,   10
> Such goodly things as you!

Why has Shakespeare chosen these words for Leontes to speak on this occasion? The answer must surely be because he wants to convey to the audience at this stage of the play a strong impression of Leontes's genuine repentance and reformation of character.

What, then, is the effect of these words? Well, the most striking thing about the diction of this passage is that so many words have a religious significance. Infection and sin are set against goodness and virtue. The first sentence is a simple prayer to the *blessed gods* to preserve the young couple from harm during their stay in Sicilia. We then learn that Leontes knows he has deserved his punishment of being left childless by the angry heavens and is aware of the contrasting goodness of others. He speaks of Polixenes, for example, as *a holy father,/A graceful gentleman* and these words describe the King of Bohemia's virtue and kindliness and indicate his state of favour in the sight of the gods. These qualities make him *sacred* and his virtue is rewarded by being *blest* with a son, who is in turn *worthy* of his father. From the last sentence it is clear that Leontes is genuinely repentant. His admiration for the innocence and the beauty of the young couple is sincere and convincing, and there is a genuine note of regret at the loss he has brought upon himself.

V

It is often maintained that adjectives and adverbs are *describing words* and that they must therefore enhance a writer's powers of description. The instruction to young children "to put plenty of *describing words,* plenty of adjectives" into a composition is fairly common. That this is not necessarily the best thing to do can be seen from the following passage. It is taken from *The Pearl* by John Steinbeck:

> At that moment the laughing Coyotito shook the rope and the scorp-
> ion fell. Kino's hand leaped to catch it, but it fell past his fingers, fell
> on the baby's shoulder, landed and struck. Then, snarling, Kino had
> it, had it in his fingers, rubbing it to a paste in his hands. He threw it
> down and beat it into the earth floor with his fist, and Coyotito   5
> screamed with pain in his box. But Kino beat and stamped the enemy
> until it was only a fragment and a moist place in the dirt. His teeth
> were bared and fury flared in his eyes and the Song of the Enemy
> roared in his ears.

The only adjectives in this passage are *laughing, earth* and *moist.* There are no adverbs. And yet the paragraph is an intensely powerful description.

How is this achieved?

The secret is in the writer's choice of nouns and verbs. Nouns and verbs lie at the heart of this powerful description, as they do with most good writing. The more you study English Literature the more you will discover that nouns and verbs have a much greater power to describe than have adjectives and adverbs, the so-called *describing words.* In many cases, and always in poor writing, adjectives and adverbs merely fill in: they don't carry the main weight of the sense as an exact and carefully chosen noun or verb can do.

If a writer chooses his nouns and verbs with great care, his description usually will not need to depend on the inclusion of adverbs and adjectives.

So it is in this example. The verbs have all the life: *shook*, the repetition of *fell, leaped*, the stabbing effect of *struck*. The verbs are the main way in which Kino's anger is described: *threw, beat, stamped, bared, flared, roared*. There is a dramatic contrast in *the laughing Coyotito* and later when *Coyotito screamed with pain*. The nouns are all self-explanatory and don't require the further aid of elaborating adjectives: *fingers, paste, fist, pain, enemy, dirt, teeth*.

VI
Our last example in this section on diction is a short poem by Wilfred Owen. It is called *Futility* and is about the death of a soldier in the First World War.

> Move him into the sun—
> Gently its touch awoke him once,
> At home, whispering of fields unsown.
> Always it woke him, even in France,
> Until this morning and this snow.   5
> If anything might rouse him now
> The kind old sun will know.
>
> Think how it wakes the seeds,—
> Woke, once, the clays of a cold star.
> Are limbs, so dear-achieved, are sides,   10
> Full-nerved—still warm—too hard to stir?
> Was it for this the clay grew tall?
> —O what made fatuous sunbeams toil
> To break earth's sleep at all?

Before commenting on the diction of the poem it is as well to clarify in a little more detail what the poem is about. In the first verse the poet asks that the dead soldier should be moved into the sunlight. Up until now the sun has always woken him and so if anything can wake him the sun will know what it is. The second verse invites the reader to consider the sun's life-giving properties and whether it can revive the dead soldier. The poet asks if life's purpose is only meaningless destruction, and questions the validity of the whole Creation.

Let us now look at the diction of the poem.

The first verse describes the sun in pleasantly sentimental terms. Its touch is gentle, it whispers (so as not to startle or offend), it is *kind* and *old* and therefore wise. Similarly, the words associated with the dead soldier are quiet and gentle and arouse pity for his plight. The instruction in the first line (*Move him into the sun*) is qualified by the next word *Gently*, with its overtones of care and tenderness. *Gently* also describes the sun's gentle touch, which woke him *at home*, where he was safe from harm. It whispered to him *of fields unsown*, fields symbolic of the promise of youth that he has not had the opportunity to fulfil. The diction of the whole verse is tranquil and considerate. The poet has created a serene atmosphere, which is deliberately to be disrupted by the changed mood of the second verse.

The first word of the second verse is again an instruction (like *Move* in the first line of the poem) and invites the reader to *Think* about the fact that all life is dependent on the sun. Then follow three questions with which the poem ends. Their tone leaves the reader in no doubt about Owen's meaning. The first question is a cry of disbelief and pity for the young man's fate. The words emphasise the precious, warm qualities of life in contrast to the harsh fact of death. The second question (*Was it for this . . .?*) is short and full of bitterness. The third expresses the futility of Creation. Owen is angered beyond measure at the loss of the young man's life. *O* in the penultimate line is an exclamation of protest and despair, and the word *fatuous* exposes the earlier description of *the kind old sun* as a complete sham, and we realize that the last two lines of the first verse are not serene and gentle at all, but bitterly sarcastic. The effect of the word *fatuous* is heightened by it being the only unusual word in the whole poem. Since it is not generally in ordinary, everyday use, it is strong enough to express the full weight of Owen's anguish and hatred. Apart from this the poem owes its success in no small measure to its simple diction. The words are direct, lucid and sincere. The sentences are simple and short.

VII

From the above examples you will see that the choice of the right words is very important. It is very important because the choice of the right words decides exactly what the writer means to say. If he chooses the wrong words, the effects he wants to create, the responses he wants to set up in the mind of the reader, will be destroyed. All good writers know this, and all good writers choose their words very carefully.

VIII

When you write about an author's diction, you are in fact revealing your own response to his words. In writing about a poem or a paragraph from a novel it is not enough to write: "I like this poem very much" or "This paragraph is very, very exciting" and leave it at that. If you do, whoever reads your work will be none the wiser, and the whole point of writing about English Literature is to write in such a way that the reader's understanding of the poem or paragraph will be deepened by reading your comments on it. So you must find reasons why the poem is good; you must find reasons why the paragraph is exciting.

A reason such as: "I like this poem about Rhyl, because I like the seaside, and especially Rhyl. We go there every year" or "I like this poem, because the man who wrote it is my uncle" is not acceptable. English Literature, remember, is concerned with the study of words, and your reasons must therefore be concerned with the words the author uses.

Concentrate on the words the author uses. Why has he chosen these particular words? How does he want you to respond? What is the effect of individual words? What is the effect of the words taken together?

There may be many reasons why a writer chooses certain words rather than others. He may choose them because they are rich in particular associations and suggest feelings or experiences he wants you to share. He may choose them because they have the appropriate sound or rhythm, or because they convey a character or describe an event or situation, or because they contain exactly the right image for his purposes.

If, then, the writer chooses a word or phrase because it contains an image he wants to use, it follows from this that it is not possible to separate diction from imagery, or, indeed, from rhythm or style, or meaning. They all go together towards the full achievement of the author's purposes. Sometimes you can discuss these matters separately. At other times you need to take all of them into account. They are kept separate in this section of the book for the sake of convenience.

IX   FOR DISCUSSION

1.   Explain carefully the different circumstances in which you would choose to use each of the following words: ooze, pour, dribble, spill, spray.

2.   Read the following passage, which is taken from the *Sunday Express* (7th March 1976), and then answer the question on it.

> Typical of I.R.A. courage that when last week a *terrorist* blew himself up with his own bomb his comrades *scarpered*, leaving their chum to be tended by *the peaceful London citizens* he had been trying to kill.
>
> Their *fellow yobboes in Donegal* must be really proud of them.
>
> For my own part I have only one regret.
>
> Isn't it a shame it was only a 1 lb. bomb? If it had been any bigger, it might have *blown up the whole bloody lot*.

Discuss what effects you think the writer intended to achieve by using each of the words and phrases which have been italicised in the above newspaper report.

3.
> This house has been *far out at sea* all night,
> The woods *crashing* through darkness, the *booming* hills,
> Winds *stampeding* the fields under the window
> *Floundering* black astride and *blinding wet* . . .

What is the collective effect (i.e. taken all together) of the italicised words in this verse from Ted Hughes's poem, *Wind*?

4.   Read the following passage, which has been slightly adapted from *Nottingham and the Mining Country* by D. H. Lawrence, and then answer the questions on it.

> The great city means beauty, dignity, and a certain splendour, but England is a mean and petty scrabble of paltry dwellings called "homes".
>
> The promoter of industry, a hundred years ago, dared to perpetrate the ugliness of my native village. And still more monstrous, prom- 5
> oters of industry today are scrabbling over the face of England with miles and square miles of red-brick "homes", like horrible scabs. And the men inside these little red rat-traps get more and more helpless, being more and more humiliated, more and more dissatisfied, like trapped rats.   10

Do away with it all, then. At no matter what cost, start in to alter it. Never mind about wages and industrial squabbling. Turn the attention elsewhere. Pull down my native village to the last brick. Plan a nucleus. Fix the focus. Make a handsome gesture of radiation from the focus. And then put up big buildings, handsome, that sweep to a 15 civic centre. And furnish them with beauty. And make an absolute clean start. Do it place by place. Make a new England. Away with little homes! Away with scrabbling pettiness and paltriness. Look at the contours of the land, and build up from these, with a sufficient nobility. The English may be mentally or spiritually developed. But as 20 citizens of splendid cities they are more ignominious than rabbits. And they nag, nag, nag all the time about politics and wages and all that, like mean narrow housewives.

(a)   When D. H. Lawrence describes the houses as being *like horrible scabs* (line 7), this suggests disease and even a sense of disgust at the way the land has been disfigured and spoiled. What do you think D. H. Lawrence intended to suggest to you by each of the following?

    (i)   dared to perpetrate (line 4)
    (ii)   little red rat-traps (line 8)
   (iii)   industrial squabbling (line 12)
   (iv)   Make a new England (line 17)
    (v)   scrabbling (line 18)

(b)   D. H. Lawrence chooses his diction carefully and makes full use of the following devices to strengthen his case:
    (i)   colloquial phrases
    (ii)   deliberate repetition
   (iii)   similes

Choose two examples of each of the above and say what effects you think the writer intended to achieve by his use of these devices.

5.   It was Miss Murdstone who was arrived, and a gloomy-looking lady she was; dark, like her brother, whom she greatly resembled in face and voice; and with very heavy eyebrows, nearly meeting over her large nose, as if, being disabled by the wrongs of her sex from wearing whiskers, she had carried them to that account. She brought with her 5 two uncompromising hard black boxes, with her initials on the lid in hard brass nails. When she paid the coachman she took her money out of a hard steel purse, and she kept the purse in a very jail of a bag which hung upon her arm by a heavy chain, and shut up like a bite. I had never, at that time, seen such a metallic lady altogether as Miss 10 Murdstone was.

The above paragraph is from *David Copperfield* by Charles Dickens. Taking each sentence in turn, discuss fully how the writer's carefully chosen diction conveys the grimness of Miss Murdstone's character.

X WRITTEN WORK

1.
> Deep in the shady sadness of a vale
> Far sunken from the healthy breath of morn,
> Far from the fiery noon, and eve's one star,
> Sat grey-hair'd Saturn, quiet as a stone,
> Still as the silence round about his lair;   5
> Forest on forest hung about his head
> Like cloud on cloud. No stir of air was there,
> Not so much life as on a summer's day
> Robs not one light seed from the feather'd grass,
> But where the dead leaf fell, there did it rest.   10
> A stream went voiceless by, still deadened more
> By reason of his fallen divinity
> Spreading a shade: the Naiad 'mid her reeds
> Press'd her cold finger closer to her lips.

The above passage is the opening of *Hyperion*, a poem by John Keats. By commenting on the diction of these lines, explain what sort of atmosphere you think the poet was seeking to achieve here.

2.   The following passage is from *Wuthering Heights* by Emily Brontë and describes a young girl as seen through the eyes of her nurse.

> She bounded before me, and returned to my side, and was off again
> like a young greyhound; and, at first, I found plenty of entertainment
> in listening to the larks singing far and near, and enjoying the sweet,
> warm sunshine; and watching her, my pet, and my delight, with her
> golden ringlets flying loose behind, and her bright cheek, as soft and
> pure in its bloom as a wild rose, and her eyes radiant with cloudless
> pleasure. She was a happy creature, and an angel, in those days.

Why has Emily Brontë chosen these words on this occasion, and what is the effect of these words? (Study the nouns and adjectives in particular.)

3.   Study the following poem by Ted Hughes. It is called *To Paint a Water Lily*.

> A green level of lily leaves
> Roofs the pond's chamber and paves
>
> The flies' furious arena: study
> These, the two minds of this lady.
>
> First observe the air's dragonfly   5
> That eats meat, that bullets by
>
> Or stands in space to take aim;
> Others as dangerous comb the hum
>
> Under the trees. There are battle-shouts
> And death-cries everywhere hereabouts   10

But inaudible, so the eyes praise
To see the colours of these flies

Rainbow their arcs, spark, or settle
Cooling like beads of molten metal

Through the spectrum. Think what worse   15
Is the pond-bed's matter of course;

Prehistoric bedragonned times
Crawl that darkness with Latin names,

Have evolved no improvements there,
Jaws for heads, the set stare,   20

Ignorant of age as of hour—
Now paint the long-necked lily-flower

Which, deep in both worlds, can be still
As a painting, trembling hardly at all

Though the dragonfly alight,   25
Whatever horror nudge her root.

The poem describes the insect life of two worlds: one, in the air above the lily leaves on
the pond's surface; the other on the bed of the pond. What contrasts are there in the
insect life of these two worlds? (Consider especially lines 11-20 and the last stanza.)

4.   The summer passed slowly like some torturing thing reluctant to let
        go. The rains came just in time, for the oily leather leaves were curling
        with crispness and turning yellow with the septic threat of death. In
        places the ground had cracked open, exposing millions of swarming
        insects to the harsh scorch glare of the sun: they ran out and withered 5
        in a few hours. It was impossible to have open the windows of the
        Company office for fear of mosquitoes and huge gnats pumped up
        with blood, but this did at least keep down the sickening stench of the
        river. It had shrunk during the summer to half its size, leaving a mass
        of grey, stagnant silt to bake and stink in the sun. The animals 10
        instinctively kept away from it.

From the above paragraph (taken from *The Turtles* by David Clarke) choose three words
or phrases which you think convey the unpleasantness of the weather or the landscape.
Explain how these words or phrases achieve their effects.

XI
To sum up. So far we have been concerned with images and diction and with their
effects upon the reader's response. Next we go on to study rhythm. But first listen to
what Ted Hughes has to say about these things. You have already read some of his
poems, he is probably our foremost modern poet, and he is worth quoting in full.

In *Poetry in the Making* he discusses the power that language has of making things real and alive and the excitement the poet feels in creating a new specimen (the poem) of the life outside his own. A poem, he says, is

> an assembly of living parts moved by a single spirit. The living parts are the words, the images, the rhythms. The spirit is the life which inhabits them when they all work together. It is impossible to say which comes first, parts or spirit. But if any of the parts are dead, if any of the words or images or rhythms do not jump to life as you read them, then the creature is going to be maimed and the spirit sickly. So, as a poet, you have to make sure that all those parts over which you have control, the words and rhythms and images, are alive. That is where the difficulties begin. Yet the rules, to begin with, are very simple. Words that live are those which we hear, like 'click' or 'chuckle', or which we see, like 'freckled' or 'veined', or which we taste, like 'vinegar' or 'sugar', or touch, like 'prickle' or 'oily', or smell, like 'tar' or 'onion'. Words which belong directly to one of the five senses. Or words which act and seem to use their muscles, like 'flick' or 'balance'.
>
> But immediately things become more difficult. 'Click' not only gives you a sound, it gives you the notion of a sharp movement, such as your tongue makes in saying 'click'. It also gives you the feel of something light and brittle, like a snapping twig. Heavy things do not click, nor do soft bendable ones. In the same way, tar not only smells strongly. It is sticky to touch, with a particular thick and choking stickiness. Also it moves, when it is soft, like a black snake, and has a beautiful black gloss. So it is with most words. They belong to several of the senses at once, as if each one had eyes, ears and tongue, or ears and fingers and a body to move with. It is this little goblin in a word which is its life and its poetry, and it is this goblin which the poet has to have under control.

From his own writing Ted Hughes goes on to illustrate what he means when he talks about language being real and alive. He writes:

> I was sitting up late one snowy night, in dreary lodgings in London. I had written nothing for a year or so but that night I got the idea I might write something and I wrote in a few minutes the following poem: the first 'animal' poem I ever wrote. Here it is—

The Thought-Fox

I imagine this midnight moment's forest:
Something else is alive
Beside the clock's loneliness
And this blank page where my fingers move.

Through the window I see no star: 5
Something more near
Though deeper within darkness
Is entering the loneliness:

Cold, delicately as the dark snow,
A fox's nose touches twig, leaf;   10
Two eyes serve a movement, that now
And again now, and now, and now

Sets neat prints into the snow
Between trees, and warily a lame
Shadow lags by stump and in hollow   15
Of a body that is bold to come

Across clearings, an eye,
A widening deepening greenness,
Brilliantly, concentratedly,
Coming about its own business   20

Till, with a sudden sharp hot stink of fox
It enters the dark hole of the head.
The window is starless still; the clock ticks,
The page is printed.

This poem does not have anything you could easily call a meaning. It is about a fox, obviously enough, but a fox that is both a fox and not a fox. What sort of a fox is it that can step right into my head where presumably it still sits, smiling to itself when the dogs bark? It is both a fox and a spirit. It is a real fox; as I read the poem I see it move, I see it setting its prints, I see its shadow going over the irregular surface of the snow. The words show me all this, bringing it nearer and nearer. It is very real to me. The words have made a body for it and given it somewhere to walk.

If, at the time of writing this poem, I had found livelier words, words that could give me much more vividly its movements, the twitch and craning of its ears, the slight tremor of its hanging tongue and its breath making little clouds, its teeth bared in the cold, the snow-crumbs dropping from its pads as it lifts each one in turn, if I could have got the words for all this, the fox would probably be even more real and alive to me now, than it is as I read the poem. Still, it is there as it is. If I had not caught the real fox there in the words I would never have saved the poem. I would have thrown it into the wastepaper basket as I have thrown so many other hunts that did not get what I was after. As it is, every time I read the poem the fox comes up again out of the darkness and steps into my head. And I suppose that long after I am gone, as long as a copy of the poem exists, every time anyone reads it the fox will get up somewhere out in the darkness and come walking towards them.

So, you see, in some ways my fox is better than an ordinary fox. It will live for ever, it will never suffer from hunger or hounds. I have it with me wherever I go. And I made it. And all through imagining it clearly enough and finding the living words.

Let us now turn to the study of rhythm.

RHYTHM

I

When you listen to a brass band in the park (as you invariably do), you are often so struck by the ooompah-pah, ooompah-pah of the euphonium playing deeply and rhythmically against the higher, twiddly bits from trumpet and cornet, that you are forced to exclaim, "How very unlike poetry! Not at all like verse!"

Your companion, alarmed, glances at you nervously, but you try to allay his (or her) evident fear.

"No, no," you say. "Fear not. The ooompah-pah drowns the twiddly bits."

Your friend goes strangely quiet. Her face grows pale and she begins to tremble with curiosity, so you continue. (It is a she, by the way, because you call her Angela.)

"Angela," you say, "the rhythm of this band is monotonously obvious. Verse is more subtle. It takes a fine and sensitive ear to hear the rhythm and the melody of words."

You make this speech to the empty air and are puzzled to find that your friend has sped away across the field and is talking to a policeman over by the trees and pointing, excitedly, in your direction.

Had Angela stayed, you would have told her more about the rhythm of words, once the concert had ended. You know she would have listened with rapture to your account of unstressed and stressed syllables, to your identification of iambic pentameters, trochees, spondees, dactylic feet, alliteration and end-stopping, and would have pondered long over the mysteries of caesura and enjambement and the secrets of masculine and feminine rhyme.

But it is not to be. Silly girl! Let her remain, then, in ignorance of assonance and onomatopoeia. The loss is hers.

A pity, too, that you will miss the rest of the band's ooomphatic performance. Angela is returning with the agitated policeman and a man in a white frock. You have time to make only a few hurried notes . . .

II

Within ourselves are many rhythms. Our hearts beat, our lungs breathe, we eat, sleep and wake according to pattern. Also we are aware of rhythms and patterns outside us in the external world: day and night, the sound of the sea, the throb of engines, clocks ticking, the cry of birds, the changing of the seasons.

Words, too, have rhythm, as you tried to explain to Angela. They have rhythm because

    (i)   they are affected by the rise and fall of speech according to stress

    (ii)   all words consist of long and/or short sounds, like the notes in music (e.g. *moon, ordinary, tap*)

You can test this quite easily by putting a random list of names into a rhythmical pattern:

> Aston Villa, Leicester City,
> Leeds United, Q.P.R.
> Glasgow Celtic, Sheffield Wednesday,
> Bristol Rovers, Crewe, Forfar.

This is a list of football clubs, but the same applies to a list of your friends' names, or to a list of flowers or vegetables. All you have to do is to arrange the words in the right order.

In ordinary speech and in prose the rhythms are irregular:

> Mr Knightley might quarrel with her, but Emma could not quarrel with herself. He was so much displeased, that it was longer than usual before he came to Hartfield again; and when they did meet, his grave looks shewed that she was not forgiven. She was sorry, but could not repent.
>
> *From* **Emma** *by Jane Austen*

But they can, and do, slip into more regular forms:

> She said she'd come, but only if you'll pick her up in Wimbledon at nine
>
> She misses Joe much more than she can say

It is this natural rhythm of living speech that the poet shapes and controls in, making his words conform to a regular rhythmical pattern. And when we talk about regular rhythms in poetry, we refer to the *metre* of a poem and we measure these rhythms in metrical feet, rather like the bars in music. The following example will make this clear to you. It is taken from *The Merchant of Venice* by William Shakespeare, and is spoken by the lovers Lorenzo and Jessica:

LOR.   The moon shines bright. In such a night as this,

When the sweet wind did gent ly kiss the trees,

And they did make no noise—in such a night

Troilus methinks mounted the Troy an walls,

And sigh'd his soul toward the Gre cian tents,

Where Cress id lay that night.

5

JESS.   In such a night

Did Thisby fearfully o'ertrip the dew,

33

˘ / | ˘ /| ˘   / | ˘   / | ˘ /
And saw the li on's shad ow ere himself,

˘   /| ˘   / |˘ / |
And ran dismayed away.

LOR.

˘ / |˘ /
In such a night

˘   / | ˘   / | ˘ /| ˘   /| ˘ /
Stood Did o with a will ow in her hand   10

˘ / | ˘   / | ˘   / | ˘   / | ˘ /
Upon the wild sea-banks, and waft her love

˘ / |˘ / | ˘   / | ˘
To come again to Carth age.

You will discover, if you count them, that there are ten syllables to each line. And you will also notice that the number of unstressed (˘) and stressed syllables (marked /) falls into a regular pattern of the ˘ / type.

This combination of an unstressed syllable followed by a stressed one is called an *Iamb*, or Iambic foot. Because there are five Iambic feet to each line, we say that these lines are written in Iambic pentameters. And because these pentameters do not rhyme, we call this form of poetry *blank verse*.

It was stated earlier that all words consist of long and/or short sounds. This is important because it is in fact the interplay of stress and vowel length that often determines the rhythm of a poem. For example, it takes longer to say:

> The long day wanes: the slow moon climbs: the deep
> Moans round with many voices
>
> *From* **Ulysses** *by Tennyson*

with its echoic, mournful music created by the long vowel sounds than to say:

> Letters of thanks, letters from banks,
> Letters of joy from girl and boy,
> Receipted bills and invitations
> To inspect new stock or visit relations
>
> *From* **Night Mail** *by W. H. Auden*

where the short vowel sounds and stressed rhymes convey the quick rhythm of the train as it speeds along the railway track.

III   WRITTEN PRACTICE

Copy out the following passage, leaving a space between each line. Then mark out the iambic rhythm according to the metrical stress. The first line is done for you.

˘   / | ˘ /| ˘   / |˘ / |˘ /
One summ er eve ning (led by her) I found
A little boat tied to a willow tree
Within a rocky cave, its usual home.

Straight I unloosed her chain, and stepping in
Pushed from the shore. It was an act of stealth   5
And troubled pleasure, nor without the voice
Of mountain-echoes did my boat move on;
Leaving behind her still, on either side,
Small circles glittering idly in the moon,
Until they melted all into one track   10
Of sparkling light.

From **The Prelude** *by William Wordsworth*

Measuring the rhythm of lines in this way is called *scansion*, but not all verse is written in iambs. There are in fact four main kinds of metrical feet, as shown in this table:

Iamb ⌣ /	⌣ / ⌣ / ⌣ / ⌣ / agáin alíve befóre remóve ⌣ / ⌣ / ⌣ / ⌣ / ⌣ / If músic bé the fóod of lóve, play ón.
Trochee / ⌣	/ ⌣ / ⌣ / ⌣ / ⌣ céiling hídden Mónday Túesday / ⌣ / ⌣ / ⌣ / ⌣ Lúcy Lócket lóst her pócket, / ⌣ / ⌣ / ⌣ Kítty Físher fóund it.
Dactyl / ⌣ ⌣	/ ⌣ ⌣ / ⌣ ⌣ / ⌣ ⌣ / ⌣ ⌣ béautiful pélican Sáturday vítamin / ⌣ ⌣ / ⌣ ⌣ / ⌣ ⌣ / Mérrily, mérrily sháll I líve nów, / ⌣ ⌣ / ⌣ ⌣ / ⌣ ⌣ / Únder the blóssom that hángs on the bóugh
Anapaest ⌣ ⌣ /	⌣ ⌣ / ⌣ ⌣ / ⌣ ⌣ / ⌣ ⌣ / expedíte interrúpt overlóok referée ⌣ ⌣ / ⌣ ⌣ / ⌣ ⌣ / ⌣ ⌣ / Not a wórd to each óther, we képt the great páce ⌣ ⌣ / ⌣ ⌣ / ⌣ ⌣ / ⌣ ⌣ / Neck by néck, stride by stríde, never chánging our pláce

Two other kinds of feet are sometimes added, but, because they can usually be resolved by scansion into one or other of the four standard feet, they are of lesser importance. They are:

Spondee / /	/ / / / / / / / armchair boat-race fireside maintain / / / / / / Slow spondee stalks; strong foot!
Amphibrach ˘ / ˘	˘ / ˘ ˘ / ˘ ˘ / ˘ ˘ / ˘ emergence illumine revealing umbrella ˘ / ˘ ˘ / ˘ ˘ / ˘ ˘ / ˘ Most friendship is feigning, most loving mere folly

In the extract from *The Merchant of Venice* note how Shakespeare varies the basic iambic rhythm by using trochees in lines 2 and 4. *Fearfully* in line 7 is a dactyl and is preceded by an amphibrach. And in the extract from *The Prelude* Wordsworth uses trochees at the start of lines 5 and 8. Departing from the regular rhythm in this way is done very often by poets for the sake of variety and interest. Iambic verse is, however, by far the most popular and the most expressive of English rhythms because of its great adaptability, and it is therefore the most important.

IV   FURTHER WRITTEN PRACTICE

1. Copy out the following verses, leaving a space between each line. Then mark out the rhythm according to the natural stress and divide the lines into metrical feet. There may be some irregularities you will need to show.

    (a)   Gracious Lord, oh bomb the Germans.
          Spare their women for Thy Sake,
      And if that is not too easy
          We will pardon Thy Mistake.
      But, gracious Lord, whate'er shall be,
      Don't let anyone bomb me.

            From **In Westminster Abbey** *by John Betjeman*

    (b)   Of Man's first disobedience, and the fruit
      Of that forbidden tree, whose mortal taste
      Brought death into the world, and all our woe,
      With loss of Eden, till one greater Man
      Restore us, and regain the blissful seat,
      Sing, heavenly Muse . . .

            From **Paradise Lost** *by John Milton*

    (c)   This day is call'd the feast of Crispian.
      He that outlives this day, and comes safe home,
      Will stand a tip-toe when this day is named,
      And rouse him at the name of Crispian.
      He that shall live this day, and see old age,   5
      Will yearly on the vigil feast his neighbours,

And say, "To-morrow is Saint Crispian."
Then will he strip his sleeve and show his scars,
And say, "These wounds I had on Crispin's day."
Old men forget; yet all shall be forgot,   10
But he'll remember, with advantages,
What feats he did that day.

From **Henry V** *by William Shakespeare*

(d) Across the wet November night
The church is bright with candlelight
     And waiting Evensong.
A single bell with plaintive strokes
Pleads louder than the stirring oaks
     The leafless lanes along.

From **Verses turned in aid of A Public Subscription (1952)**
towards the restoration of the Church of St. Katherine
Chiselhampton, Oxon *by John Betjeman*

2.   Put a line, thus (—) over every long vowel sound in the following passage:

Music that brings sweet sleep down from the blissful skies.
Here are cool mosses deep,
And thro' the moss the ivies creep,
And in the stream the long-leaved flowers weep,
And from the craggy ledge the poppy hangs in sleep.

From **The Lotus-Eaters** *by Tennyson*

V FINDING OUT

1.   Find out what is meant by each of the following: (i) an alexandrine, (ii) a dactylic
tetrameter, (iii) elision, (iv) masculine and feminine endings, (v) quatrains, (vi) heroic
couplets, (vii) free verse.

2.   What is the difference between alliteration and assonance? Give two examples of
each.

3.   What is onomatopoeia? Give an example.

4.   What is meant by (i) enjambement, (ii) end-stopped lines?

5.   In lines of four feet or more, in addition to the natural pause of the voice at the end
of a line of poetry, there is another pause which occurs somewhere within the line. This
pause is known as the *caesura*, and, by moving the position of the caesura, a poet can
give great variety to the cadence of his verses. Demonstrate this by finding the position
of the caesura in each of the lines already quoted from *The Merchant of Venice, The
Prelude* and *Henry V*.

6.   (i) Why is bear/fear called an eye-rhyme? (ii) What is internal rhyme? (iii) What is para-rhyme? (iv) What is the difference between masculine and feminine rhyme? (v) What is complete rhyme?

7.   Define the following poetic forms: (i) sonnet, (ii) ode, (iii) elegy, (iv) epic. Name one famous example of each form.

VI

You will see from what has been said so far, and from what you have learned from your own researches, that rhythm can be a highly technical subject with many specialist terms. Knowledge of this sort is valuable if it helps you to see that the poet is a craftsman, exercising a conscious control and making something; but there is no merit merely in pointing out that a poet is using a trochaic metre or that he uses repetition (e.g. "In such a night") unless you relate his use of these devices to his purposes. You need to say what the effects of a poet's rhythms are, in the same way as you have learned to describe the effects of an author's diction.

VII

Here are two examples. The first is from *Much Ado About Nothing*. Claudio, mistakenly believing that his bride (Hero) has been unfaithful to him, denounces her before her father (Leonato) and the assembled company who have gathered in the church to witness their marriage. Hero blushes with the deep hurt and disgrace of this public and unjust shaming.

> There, Leonato, take her back again:
> Give not this rotten orange to your friend;
> She's but the sign and semblance of her honour.
> Behold how like a maid she blushes here!
> O, what authority and show of truth   5
> Can cunning sin cover itself withal!
> Comes not that blood as modest evidence
> To witness simple virtue? Would you not swear,
> All you that see her, that she were a maid,
> By these exterior shows? But she is none: 10
> She knows the heat of a luxurious bed;
> Her blush is guiltiness, not modesty.

The natural stresses of the first line fall on *There, take* and *back,* so underlining the strength of Claudio's feeling. *There, Leonato,* has a contemptuous ring, the pause after each word (shown by the punctuation) lending weight to Claudio's scorn. The verse then builds up through two exclamations (in line 4 and lines 5-6) and two parallel questions (in lines 7-10) to a rhetorical and emphatic answer: *But she is none.* This answer is definite and short and comes with the determination of a judgement. Most of the lines are end-stopped and the caesura is used strongly in the last five lines, giving a measured conviction to the rhythm of the verse. The passage thus has a deliberate and balanced design which can be detected in the rhythm. The verse is that of carefully controlled and convincing statement. It is as if Claudio has planned and rehearsed it all, as indeed he has.

The second example is from *Hamlet*. Hamlet himself speaks these lines. He is disillusioned and upset because his mother has remarried within a very short time of his father's death. Hamlet thought the world of his father and is all the more disturbed that his mother has now married a man whom he despises. Tortured, he thinks how desirable it would be to die, to commit suicide; and he meditates upon the hollowness and corruption of the world.

> O, that this too too solid flesh would melt,
> Thaw, and resolve itself into a dew!
> Or that the Everlasting had not fix'd
> His canon 'gainst self-slaughter! Oh God! God!
> How weary, stale, flat, and unprofitable,   5
> Seem to me all the uses of this world!
> Fie on't! Ah, fie! 'tis an unweeded garden,
> That grows to seed; things rank and gross in nature
> Possess it merely. That it should come to this!
> But two months dead! Nay, not so much, not two.   10
> So excellent a king that was to this
> Hyperion to a satyr; so loving to my mother,
> That he might not beteem the winds of heaven
> Visit her face too roughly.

Hamlet's horror at the marriage is clearly revealed. The movement of the verse is suitably broken, as befits the disturbed state of mind of the speaker. For example, the adjectives in line 5 are separated by heavy pauses and are thus given emphasis. Line 6 has no obvious caesura and is delivered in a weary monotone. *Fie on't! Ah, fie!* in contrast is spoken with some force, showing Hamlet's disgust. He almost spits out the words. The long pause after *merely* in line 9 shows the speaker lost in thought, reflecting on the situation. The meaning of *That it should come to this!* is given by the next exclamatory phrase, *But two months dead!* which, in turn, receives a qualifying after-thought, *Nay, not so much, not two.* In this way the verse is ongoing and spontaneous, revealing Hamlet's thoughts as they occur to him. The enjambement of lines 3 and 4 and of lines 8 and 9 adds a prosaic quality to the verse, reducing its rhythmic rise and fall to a level which is flat and dispirited. Even in the quicker rhythms of lines 11-14 there is no majestic or elevating sweep: the bitterness of Hamlet's thought is so strongly presented.

From these examples it should be clear to you that sounds and rhythms can never be considered in isolation (apart perhaps from nonsense verse). The sound of a word is also a meaning, and anything you write about rhythm must involve the meaning of the words and the way they are meant to be sounded in order to reveal that meaning.

VIII

What is the poet's intention? Is he trying to create a melodious effect by means of a pleasing sound-pattern? Or are the words harsh, suggesting tension, or hardness, or noise, or cruelty? Or are they soft, suggesting comfort, or drowsiness, or peace? Do the words move quickly or slowly? What words are emphasised and why? What contribution is made by the pauses? How should the words be spoken? How does the rhythm fit in with the subject-matter? These are the sorts of questions you must ask yourself, and try to answer.

IX FOR DISCUSSION

1. The following poems and extracts have been chosen because any thoughtful discussion about them will need to take account of their differing rhythmical properties. Compare and contrast them, bearing in mind what you have learned in this section, and using the questions listed above as a general guide.

    (a) Do you remember an Inn,
Miranda?
Do you remember an Inn?
And the tedding and the spreading
Of the straw for a bedding,   5
And the fleas that tease in the High Pyrenees,
And the wine that tasted of the tar?
And the cheers and the jeers of the young muleteers
(Under the dark of the vine verandah)?
Do you remember an Inn, Miranda,   10
Do you remember an Inn?
And the cheers and the jeers of the young muleteers
Who hadn't got a penny,
And who weren't paying any,
And the hammer at the doors and the Din?   15
And the Hip! Hop! Hap!
Of the clap
Of the hands to the twirl and swirl
Of the girl gone chancing,
Glancing,   20
Dancing,
Backing and advancing,
Snapping of the clapper to the spin
Out and in—
And the Ting, Tong, Tang of the guitar!   25
Do you remember an Inn,
Miranda,
Do you remember an Inn?

      Never more,
Miranda,   30
Never more.
Only the high peaks hoar:
And Aragon a torrent at the door.
No sound
In the walls of the Halls where falls   35
The tread
Of the feet of the dead to the ground.
No sound:
Only the boom
Of the far Waterfall like Doom.   40

                                    Tarantella *by Hilaire Belloc*

(b)   Gr-r-r—there go, my heart's abhorrence!
          Water your damned flower-pots, do!
       If hate killed men, Brother Lawrence,
          God's blood, would not mine kill you!
       What? your myrtle-bush wants trimming?   5
          Oh, that rose has prior claims—
       Needs its leaden vase filled brimming?
          Hell dry you up with its flames!

       At the meal we sit together:
          Salve tibi! I must hear   10
       Wise talk of the kind of weather,
          Sort of season, time of year:
       Not a plenteous cork-crop: scarcely
          Dare we hope oak-galls, I doubt:
       What's the Latin name for "parsley"?   15
          What's the Greek name for Swine's Snout?

From **Soliloquy of the Spanish Cloister** *by Robert Browning*

(c)   Tread lightly, she is near
          Under the snow,
       Speak gently, she can hear
          The daisies grow.

       All her bright golden hair   5
          Tarnished with rust,
       She that was young and fair
          Fallen to dust.

       Lily-like, white as snow,
          She hardly knew   10
       She was a woman, so
          Sweetly she grew.

       Coffin-board, heavy stone,
          Lie on her breast,
       I vex my heart alone,   15
          She is at rest.

       Peace, peace, she cannot hear
          Lyre or sonnet,
       All my life's buried here,
          Heap earth upon it.   20

Requiescat *by Oscar Wilde*

(d) My aspens dear, whose airy cages quelled,
     Quelled or quenched in leaves the leaping sun,
     All felled, felled, are all felled;
        Of a fresh and following folded rank
           Not spared, not one   5
              That dandled a sandalled
           Shadow that swam or sank
     On meadow and river and wind-wandering weed-winding bank.

From **Binsey Poplars** *(felled 1879) by Gerard Manley Hopkins*

(e) Dry clash'd his harness in the icy caves
     And barren chasms, and all to left and right
     The bare black cliff clang'd round him, as he based
     His feet on juts of slippery crag that rang
     Sharp-smitten with the dint of armed heels—   5
     And on a sudden, lo! the level lake,
     And the long glories of the winter moon.

From **Morte d'Arthur** *by Tennyson*

2.   Because the rhythms of prose are so varied and irregular, it is not possible to discuss prose rhythms in the same way as those of poetry. There is no definite pattern to speak of in prose. Yet prose can make very different sounds, with rhythm—or the absence of rhythm—playing a significant part. Consider these examples:

(a) Coat the veal in beaten egg and then in breadcrumbs. Melt 2 oz.
butter and fry the veal until golden-brown and evenly coloured. Drain
and place in a rigid foil dish. Add the remaining butter to the frying
pan. Seed the peppers, slice roughly and fry for a few mins., spoon
them over the meat. Heat the white sauce until boiling; boil for 1-2
min., but remove from the heat before adding the sherry. Blend fully,
and add some freshly milled pepper.

From GOOD HOUSEKEEPING **Home Freezer Cook Book**
Extract from recipe 'Veal in Sherry Sauce'.

(b) "Now, boys, this is a new half. Take care what you're about, in
this new half. Come fresh up to the lessons, I advise you, for I come
fresh up to the punishment. I won't flinch. It will be of no use your
rubbing yourselves; you won't rub the marks out that I shall give you.
Now get to work, every boy!"   5

When this dreadful exordium was over, Mr Creakle came to where I
sat, and told me that if I were famous for biting, he was famous for
biting, too. He then showed me the cane, and asked me what I thought
of *that*, for a tooth? Was it a sharp tooth, hey? Was it a double tooth,
hey? Had it a deep prong, hey? Did it bite, hey? Did it bite? At every 10
question he gave me a fleshy cut with it that made me writhe; so I was
very soon in tears.

From **David Copperfield** *(slightly adapted) by Charles Dickens*

(c) Now Melkor began the delving and building of a vast fortress, deep under Earth, beneath dark mountains where the beams of Illuin were cold and dim. That stronghold was named Utumno. And though the Valar knew naught of it as yet, nonetheless the evil of Melkor and the blight of his hatred flowed out thence, and the Spring of Arda was 5 marred. Green things fell sick and rotted, and rivers were choked with weeds and slime, and fens were made, rank and poisonous, the breeding place of flies; and forests grew dark and perilous, the haunts of fear; and beasts became monsters of horn and ivory and dyed the earth with blood.   10

From **The Silmarillion** *by J. R. R. Tolkien*

(d) They shot the six cabinet ministers at half-past six in the morning against the wall of a hospital. There were pools of water in the court-yard. There were dead leaves on the paving of the court-yard. It rained hard. All the shutters of the hospital were nailed shut. One of the ministers was sick with typhoid. Two soldiers carried him down- 5 stairs and out into the rain. They tried to hold him up against the wall but he sat down in a puddle of water. The other five stood very quietly against the wall. Finally the officer told the soldiers it was no good trying to make him stand up. When they fired the first volley he was sitting down in the water with his head on his knees.   10

From **In Our Time** *from* **The First Forty-nine Stories** *by*
Ernest Hemingway

These extracts are obviously very different, but in what ways? To help you discover something of the different rhythms and sounds in these passages, consider the following questions:

(i) For which one of these passages is the spoken word the most important, and for which one is it least so? Why?

(ii) Part of one passage has what might be described as "a flowing rhythm". Which passage is this, and what makes it "flow" in this way?

(iii) The writer of passage (b) uses certain rhythmical devices—exclamation, repetition, repeated questions, stress on certain words—in order to portray Mr Creakle. Identify examples of these rhythmical devices and say what they reveal of Mr Creakle's feelings and character.

(iv) What do you notice about the length of the sentences in passage (d)? What effects are achieved by writing in this way? How do the writer's purposes differ from those of the writer of passage (a)?

X
In your discussions of the rhythms and sounds of these poems and prose passages it is certain that you will have been unable to avoid some discussion also of the writers' imagery and diction, and, at the heart of everything, the writers' meaning.

Imagery, diction and rhythm cannot be separated from the meaning, nor can they be separated from the same thing. They all go together. And it is to these literary terms, *style* and *meaning*, that we now must, finally and briefly, turn.

STYLE

I

The American poet Robert Frost once said, "All the fun's in how you say a thing." Style is not an easy term to define, but Frost's brief definition is as good as any. Style is "how you say a thing." In other words, style is the way in which something is written or said, as distinct from its subject matter.

In talking about style you have to consider all those things that play their part in creating the way in which something is written or said: the imagery, the diction, the length of sentences and their structure, and the rise and fall of the words (the rhythm).

It is because style is so inextricably bound up with these other things that it is almost impossible to isolate it as a separate topic for discussion. Furthermore, the style a writer adopts depends partly on his own personality but very largely on what he has to say and what his purposes are. It follows that style and subject matter should match each other appropriately. For example, a scientific report will obviously be much more formal and objective in style than a poem which is trying to convey an intensely personal and moving experience (like Jon Silkin's poem, *Death of a Son,* for instance).

Just how important it is to choose an appropriate style can be seen by examining the following three sentences, which all say the same thing but in different ways:

> My dear parent is going to his heavenly home

> My father is dying

> The old fella's on his way out

Though these sentences say the same thing, how they say it—*the style*—is very different in each. The first one is unduly sentimental and rather pompous. It has a falsely religious ring to it because, in striving to be dignified, it is overstated. The second one is plain and simple. It doesn't try to disguise the unpleasant fact of death by using a gentler expression like "passing away". Its simplicity gives it a sincerity and a dignity which are lacking in the first sentence, and, according to how it was said, it would be capable of conveying immeasurable grief in a way which is not possible with the other two. The third sentence is ludicrously insensitive, the use of slang suggesting the speaker's lack of respect or concern for his father.

As a general rule, then, when it comes to your own writing, it is best to say what you have to say in a plain and simple form. It is almost always better to write "He died poor" than to write "He expired in indigent circumstances."

Much does depend on circumstances, of course. "The old fella's on his way out" could be used with full justification by a playwright who wanted to convey the brash, callous nature of one of his characters. Similarly, "My father is dying" could be used to show a coldly unemotional temperament. How might the first example be used?

II FOR DISCUSSION

1.   How does the addition of the word "please" affect the style of the following remark?

> Fish, chips, and a cup of coffee.

2.   Reword the following sentences in the simplest possible form:

> (a)   He was elevated to the peerage.

> (b)   In the vicinity of my abode the town's democratically-elected representatives recently purchased several uninhabited dwellings which they intend to raze to the ground and erect thereon a manu-factory.

> (c)   Despite the adverse climatic conditions appertaining to the Sab-bath we achieved a complete pedestrian circuition of the city of Chester within the duration of the morning.

III

Let us now consider three passages which are very different in style.

> (a)   The development since World War II of a highly complex system of international cooperation and interaction among the advanced industrial democracies is of great significance, not only for them, but for the world as a whole. Economically, politically, militarily, and (to an increasing extent) socially and ideologically, Western Europe, 5 North America, Japan, Australia, and New Zealand have found their vital interests—both within this grouping and vis-à-vis the rest of the world—intersecting in a web of steadily increasing interdependence.
>
> *From* **The Global Significance of the Evolving Atlantic-Pacific System** *by James Robert Huntley, published in* **Nato Review**, *December 1977*

This first passage consists of two fairly long and involved sentences which begin to develop an argument. The author's views are stated with authority and conviction, as shown by his educated vocabulary and complex phrasing (*international cooperation and interaction, vis-à-vis, steadily increasing interdependence*). Apart from the word *web* there is no imagery: the passage is written in the language of political commentary. The style is technical and abstract. It is not for the common reader.

> (b)   Even though large tracts of Europe and many old and famous states have fallen or may fall into the grip of the Gestapo and all the odious apparatus of Nazi rule, we shall not flag or fail. We shall fight in France, we shall fight in the seas and oceans, we shall fight with growing confidence and growing strength in the air; we shall defend 5 our island, whatever the cost may be. We shall fight on the beaches,

we shall fight on the landing-grounds, we shall fight in the fields and in the streets; we shall never surrender; and even if, which I do not for a moment believe, this Island or a large part of it were subjugated and starving, then our Empire beyond the seas, armed and guarded by the 10 British Fleet, would carry on the struggle, until, in God's good time, the New World, with all its power and might, steps forth to the rescue and the liberation of the old.

> *From* **A Speech to Parliament**, *4 June 1940, by*
> *Winston Churchill*

This passage is written in the style of oratory, its purpose being to uplift and inspire all its hearers in defiance of the enemy. The brief, repeated exclamation, *we shall fight*, drives the message home; and the catalogue of places—France, the seas and oceans, the air, the beaches, the landing-grounds, the fields and streets—suggests the totality of the defiance. The reference to *our island* has a patriotic appeal which contrasts sharply with *the odious apparatus of Nazi rule*, and the further references to *our Empire* and *the British Fleet* suggest other sources of power and consolidated strength. The alliteration of, for example, *fall into the grip of the Gestapo, flag or fail* and *fight* adds a rhythmical emphasis to the meaning. In other words, the paragraph contains a number of stylistic and rhetorical devices—such as repetition, rhythm, concrete images, variety of length of phrase—which the speaker uses deliberately in order to reinforce his meaning and make his message plain.

> (c)   I blew into this big smoke Thursday from—but I must clam up about where I left the tin bird. And here I am pen-pushing to you in a plush lobster palace, or so you'd think it from the out-of-sight prices. Yet all the dish-juggler chucked at us was a splash of red noise, a slab of crippled beef on a load of hay, and a plate of wop-worms. This may call itself a swell dine-wine-dancery but I've eaten better at a quick and filthy in my time.

> *From an imaginary letter home by an American airman stationed in England, quoted by Desmond MacCarthy in a review of* **The American Thesaurus of Slang: A Complete Reference Book of Colloquial Speech** *by Lester V. Berrey and Melville van den Bark*

The extensive use of American slang in this passage makes it amusing. It is not quite clear what *red noise* and *wop-worms* are, though one could hazard a guess, but *a quick and filthy* is a vivid and original expression. The whole passage has a colourful style, but the slang is obviously, and deliberately, overdone for the sake of the humorous effect.

IV   FOR DISCUSSION

The following poems and passages should be discussed with your teacher. Pay particular attention to qualities of style. The first passage is spoken by Linda, the wife of Willy Loman, to her sons, who seem not to understand their father's condition. Linda believes her husband's occasionally strange behaviour and lapses of memory are caused by his firm's rejection of him and by exhaustion brought on by age and overwork.

1.   LINDA: I don't say he's a great man. Willy Loman never made a lot of money. His name was never in the paper. He's not the finest character that ever lived. But he's a human being, and a terrible thing is happening to him. So attention must be paid. He's not to be allowed to fall into his grave like an old dog. Attention, attention must be finally paid to such a person.

From **Death of a Salesman** *by Arthur Miller*

2.   Napoleon I, whose career had the quality of a duel against the whole of Europe, disliked duelling between the officers of his army. The great military emperor was not a swashbuckler, and had little respect for tradition.

Nevertheless, a story of duelling, which became a legend in the army, 5 runs through the epic of imperial wars. To the surprise and admiration of their fellows, two officers, like insane artists trying to gild refined gold or paint the lily, pursued a private contest through the years of universal carnage. They were officers of cavalry, and their connexion with the high-spirited but fanciful animal which carries 10 men into battle seems particularly appropriate. It would be difficult to imagine for heroes of this legend two officers of infantry of the line, for example, whose fantasy is tamed by much walking exercise, and whose valour necessarily must be of a more plodding kind. As to gunners or engineers, whose heads are kept cool on a diet of mathema- 15 tics, it is simply unthinkable.

From **The Duel** *by Joseph Conrad*

3.   *A coffee stall. A* BARMAN *and an old* NEWSPAPER SELLER. *The* BARMAN *leans on his counter, the* OLD MAN *stands with tea. Silence.*

MAN:	You was a bit busy earlier.
BARMAN:	Ah.
MAN:	Round about ten.
BARMAN:	Ten, was it?
MAN:	About then.
	(Pause.)
	I passed by here about then.
BARMAN:	Oh yes?
MAN:	I noticed you were doing a bit of trade.
	(Pause.)
BARMAN:	Yes, trade was very brisk about ten.
MAN:	Yes, I noticed.
	(Pause.)
	I sold my last one about then. Yes. About nine forty-five.
BARMAN:	Sold your last then, did you?
MAN:	Yes, my last *Evening News* it was. Went about twenty to ten.
	(Pause.)
BARMAN:	*Evening News*, was it?

5

10

15

47

MAN: Yes.
          (*Pause.*)
          Sometimes it's the *Star* is the last to go.
BARMAN: Ah.
MAN: Or the . . . Whatsisname.
BARMAN: *Standard*.   20
MAN: Yes.
          (*Pause.*)
          All I had left tonight was the *Evening News*.
          (*Pause.*)
BARMAN: Then that went, did it?
MAN: Yes.
          (*Pause.*)

From **Last to Go** *by Harold Pinter*

4.   It was my thirtieth year to heaven
     Woke to my hearing from harbour and neighbour wood
        And the mussel pooled and the heron
           Priested shore
        The morning beckon   5
     With water praying and call of seagull and rook
     And the knock of sailing boats on the net webbed wall
        Myself to set foot
           That second
     In the still sleeping town and set forth.   10

From **Poem in October** *by Dylan Thomas*

5.   **Death of a Son** (who died in a mental hospital, aged one)

Something has ceased to come along with me.
Something like a person: something very like one.
   And there was no nobility in it
      Or anything like that.

Something was there like a one-year-   5
Old house, dumb as stone. While the near buildings
   Sang like birds and laughed
      Understanding the pact

They were to have with silence. But he
Neither sang nor laughed. He did not bless silence   10
   Like bread, with words.
      He did not forsake silence.

But rather, like a house in mourning
Kept the eye turned to watch the silence while
   The other houses like birds   15
      Sang around him.

And the breathing silence neither
Moved nor was still.

I have seen stones: I have seen brick
But this house was made up of neither bricks nor stone   20
    But a house of flesh and blood
       With flesh of stone

And bricks for blood. A house
Of stones and blood in breathing silence with the other
    Birds singing crazy on its chimneys.   25
       But this was silence,

This was something else, this was
Hearing and speaking though he was a house drawn
    Into silence, this was
       Something religious in his silence,   30

Something shining in his quiet,
This was different this was altogether something else:
    Though he never spoke, this
       Was something to do with death.

And then slowly the eye stopped looking   35
Inward. The silence rose and became still.
The look turned to the outer place and stopped,
    With the birds still shrilling around him.
       And as if he could speak

He turned over on his side with this one year   40
Red as a wound
He turned over as if he could be sorry for this
And out of his eyes two great tears rolled, like stones, and he died.

by Jon Silkin

V FINDING OUT

George Orwell, in his novel *Nineteen eighty-four*, invented a new language called
Newspeak. *Oldthinkers unbellyfeel Ingsoc* is an example of it.

Study Part I Chapters IV and V of this novel and the novel's Appendix and find out:

(a) what this new language was and what its main purposes and characteristics
were;

(b) what is meant by the classification of Newspeak words into the A, B and C
vocabularies.

Compile your findings into a report of not more than two pages in length.

VI WRITTEN WORK

Six passages are printed below. Read them very carefully and then answer the questions.

(a)   O Lord our Lord, how excellent is thy name in all the earth! who hast set thy glory above the heavens . . .
   When I consider thy heavens, the work of thy fingers, the moon and the stars which thou hast ordained;
   What is man, that thou art mindful of him?

From **Psalm 8**

(b)   The animals huddled about Clover, not speaking. The knoll where they were lying gave them a wide prospect across the countryside. Most of Animal Farm was within their view—the long pasture stretching down to the main road, the hayfield, the spinney, the drinking pool, the ploughed fields where the young wheat was thick 5 and green, and the red roofs of the farm buildings with the smoke curling from the chimneys. It was a clear spring evening. The grass and the bursting hedges were gilded by the level rays of the sun. Never had the farm—and with a kind of surprise they remembered that it was their own farm, every inch of it their own property—appeared to 10 the animals so desirable a place. As Clover looked down the hillside her eyes filled with tears.

From **Animal Farm** *by George Orwell*

(c)   "The apples themselves are the very finest sort for baking, beyond a doubt; all from Donwell—some of Mr Knightley's most liberal supply. He sends us a sack every year; and certainly there never was such a keeping apple anywhere as one of his trees—I believe there is two of them. My mother says the orchard was always famous in her 5 younger days. But I was really quite shocked the other day—for Mr Knightley called one morning, and Jane was eating these apples, and we talked about them and said how much she enjoyed them, and he asked whether we were not got to the end of our stock. 'I am sure you must be,' said he, 'and I will send you another supply; for I have a 10 great many more than I can ever use. William Larkins let me keep a larger quantity than usual this year. I will send you some more, before they get good for nothing.' So I begged he would not—for really as to ours being gone, I could not absolutely say that we had a great many left—it was but half a dozen indeed; but they should be all kept for 15 Jane; and I could not at all bear that he should be sending us more, so liberal as he had been already; and Jane said the same."

From **Emma** *by Jane Austen*

(d)   Bright at last close of a dark day the sun shines out at last and goes down. Sitting quite still at valley window normally turn head now and see it the sun low in the southwest sinking. Even get up certain

moods and go stand by western window quite still watching it sink and
then the afterglow. Always quite still some reason some time past this 5
hour at open window facing south in small upright wicker chair with
armrests. Eyes stare out unseeing till first movement some time past
close though unseeing still while still light. Quite still again then all
quite quiet apparently till eyes open again while still light though less.
Normally turn head now ninety degrees to watch sun which if already 10
gone then fading afterglow. Even get up certain moods and go stand
by western window till quite dark and even some evenings some
reason long after. Eyes then open again while still light and close again
in what if not quite a single movement almost.

From **Still** *by Samuel Beckett*

(e)   "Anyway it was Spring, tadpole time, and it's swarming with
tadpoles down there in Spring. Edges of t'pond are all black with 'em,
and me and this other kid started to catch 'em. It was easy, all you did,
you just put your hands together and scooped a handful of water up
and you'd got a handful of tadpoles. Anyway we were mucking about 5
with 'em, picking 'em up and chucking 'em back and things, and we
were on about taking some home, but we'd no jam jars. So this kid,
Reggie, says, 'Take thi wellingtons off and put some in there, they'll
be all right 'til tha gets home.' So I took 'em off and we put some water
in 'em and then we started to put taddies in 'em."   10

From **A Kestrel for a Knave** *by Barry Hines*

(f)   Mr Caldwell was born 21 December 1896, on Staten Island, New
York City. His father was the Reverend John Wesley Caldwell, a
graduate of Princeton University and the Union Theological Semi-
nary, New York. Upon graduation from the latter place he entered the
Presbyterian ministry, making his the fifth generation of clergymen 5
supplied by the Caldwell family to this denomination. His wife, née
Phyllis Harthorne, was of Southern extraction, hailing from the near
environs of Nashville, Tennessee.

From **The Centaur** *by John Updike*

1.   The style of three of the above passages could be described as follows:
   (i)   child's talk; spontaneous and colloquial; evidence of regional accent
   (ii)   poetic; highly individualistic; mellow and elegaic; repetitive; difficult to
understand
   (iii)   clean style; clear-cut, pleasant description; easy to read; accurately observed
detail

Assign these three descriptions to their appropriate passages and justify your choices by
giving reasoned comments on the diction, imagery, sentence structure and rhythm of
the passages you select.

2.   Write a brief comment on the differing styles of each of the three remaining
passages.

MEANING

I

Words work in many ways. As we have seen, the way something is written or said is bound to affect its meaning. Expression is an integral part of the meaning.

Often it is a major part of the meaning. This is especially true of the spoken word, where facial expressions, gestures and the tone of voice all give the listener clear indications as to how the words are to be taken. For example, *Pass the butter dish* may really mean: "I'm furious with you for staying out so late last night." *Have you seen the scissors?* may not be a straightforward enquiry. It could easily mean: "What have you done with them?" or "Someone has damaged them beyond repair!" It all depends on how it is said. The whole meaning is altered by the tone (and the context) in which the statement (or question or command) is spoken.

So you see, we use words to communicate, but, whether we are aware of it or not, we communicate not only meanings to each other but also feelings and attitudes.

II

When we try to understand the meaning of written words, we do not have the help that is given by a speaker's facial expressions, gestures or tone of voice. The matter is further complicated by the fact that the meaning of something can work on different levels. The novel *Animal Farm*, for example, is sub-titled A FAIRY STORY, and on one level it is just that. It can be read quite easily by young children who think of it as a story of how some pigs take over a farm. But to the adult mind the novel is a satire upon the Russian Revolution, with the various animals representing important political figures, and various situations in the novel standing for historical places and events.

III

Very often we have to "read between the lines", as the saying is, in order to discover the meaning which is implied rather than stated openly. Here is an example. It is called *Burning Children* and it appeared in *The Listener* on 5 November 1970.

> Today is Burning Children Day. Tonight hospitals may expect their traditional tribute of charred youth. Last week the BBC showed again its public-spirited horror film, allegedly responsible for cutting the number of victims by half in 1969, and upholders of the sport clashed with their killjoy opponents in *Remember, Remember* (BBC 1). The 5 firework manufacturers and friends reasoned weightily. Casualties occur among children of uneducated and irresponsible parents, so matter less. Anyway, a mere thousand children are burned annually, and who on that account would tamper with the profits of the Union of Retail Tobacconists? If we mollycoddle children by denying them 10 gunpowder, we shall soon be trying to stop motorists running them down. Where will it end? Have not the kindly manufacturers gone to the expense of making a five-minute film on firework safety? This potent precaution was shown. Sure enough, there was a family, quite unscorched, advertising fireworks as merrily as could be. The Home 15 Secretary, it transpired, had declined an invitation to join the debaters since "it was not presently a proper time to have this discussion."

The author's attack—it was written by John Carey—upon the manufacturers of fireworks is all the more effective for being so subtle. By pretending to defend them and to be on their side of the argument he is able to show just how ridiculous their views are.

This device of apparently saying the opposite of what you really mean is called *irony*. (In its most elementary form it is called sarcasm!)

IV

Sometimes the meaning of a poem or a paragraph is obscure because the writer uses difficult imagery or diction or symbols which can have widely differing interpretations. Blake's poem, *The Sick Rose*, is a good example of the latter:

> O Rose thou art sick.
> The invisible worm,
> That flies in the night
> In the howling storm,
>
> Has found out thy bed   5
> Of crimson joy:
> And his dark secret love
> Does thy life destroy.

What this poem means can only be discovered by trying to decide what the symbols stand for. Does this next poem, by Edwin Morgan, "mean" anything? What do you make of the last word of the poem?

> not to be deflected
> the arrow, puffed up
> speeding busily
> straight to its
>   targjx

Philip Larkin's short poem *Days*, though using very simple diction, can be difficult to understand:

> What are days for?
> Days are where we live.
> They come, they wake us
> Time and time over.
> They are to be happy in.   5
> Where can we live but days?
>
> Ah, solving that question
> Brings the priest and the doctor
> In their long coats
> Running over the fields.   10

Any attempt to decide what this poem means must take very careful account of the imagery in the last verse. What do the priest and the doctor represent? What question are they wanting to solve? Why are they running, and where to?

V FINDING OUT

1. Your understanding and appreciation of the written word will be enhanced if you know something about the figures of speech in English. *Simile* and *metaphor* have already been dealt with in the section on images, but there are others: *innuendo*, for example.

Innuendo is a figure of speech where the meaning is not plainly stated but merely hinted at. It is usually an insinuation of the worst kind, for example:

Roger Wilbraham worked for me for two years and during that time
he was often sober.

Define, and give two examples of each of the following major figures of speech: personification, antithesis, hyperbole, allegory, paradox, epigram, oxymoron, bathos, litotes, euphemism, synecdoche, zeugma.

2.   What is (i) ambiguity, (ii) parody, (iii) cliché? Give two examples of each.

3.   Make sure you understand the difference between *denotation* and *connotation*.

VI   FOR DISCUSSION

1.   Which of the following would you expect to be *denotative* and which *connotative*? (i) a consumer report on refrigerators, (ii) a love song, (iii) a poem about a relative, (iv) an article in *The New Scientist*, (v) an obituary, (vi) a recipe, (vii) a receipt, (viii) a hymn.

2.   *Shades of meaning*. Explain the different uses of the following groups of words: (i) girl, maiden, female; (ii) poor, impecunious, broke; (iii) dislike, shun, abominate; (iv) hopeful, enthusiastic, exultant; (v) salesman, pedlar, vendor.

3.   How many different meanings can you find for each of the following words? (i) board, (ii) home, (iii) fly, (iv) stage, (v) close.

4.   Identify the sports with which the following expressions are associated: (i) game and second set, (ii) winning post, (iii) deep third man, (iv) parallel bars, (v) forward pass, (vi) gone to earth, (vii) home base, (viii) birdie three, (ix) short corner, (x) men's slalom.

VII   WRITTEN WORK

1.   In the following extract from Peter Shaffer's play *Five-Finger Exercise* you need to think very carefully about the gestures, expressions and tone of voice of each of the three speakers. Only by deciding exactly how their speeches should be said will you arrive at an accurate assessment of their characters.

> *Stanley and Louise are waiting for their son Clive, who is a student, to join them at breakfast. Stanley looks at his watch.*

STANLEY:	Is Clive coming down at all today?
LOUISE:	I've left him to sleep. He was very late last night.
STANLEY:	What time did he get in?
LOUISE:	I haven't the faintest idea. I didn't wait up for him.
STANLEY:	That's a wonder.

Clive enters hesitantly, conscious of being very late.

CLIVE:	Good morning.
STANLEY:	Good afternoon. What do you think this place is—a hotel?
CLIVE:	I'm sorry.
LOUISE:	(*being extra friendly and welcoming for Stanley's benefit*): Good morning, Jou-Jou! How did you sleep, darling?
CLIVE:	Very well, thank you.
LOUISE:	Don't I get a kiss this morning? (*He kisses her.*) That's better . . . (*looking at the plate of eggs she has placed before him*) I'm afraid those eggs are quite horrid now. Let me make you some more.

54

CLIVE:	No, these are all right. Really.
LOUISE:	It's no trouble, darling.
CLIVE:	They are fine, thank you, mother.
STANLEY:	Why were you so late last night?
CLIVE:	I—I got involved. In London. I had some work to do. 20
STANLEY:	Work?
CLIVE:	I promised to review something. It's going to be printed.
STANLEY:	Oh? In *The Times*, I suppose?
CLIVE:	No, it's more of a magazine actually. It's not really famous. 25
STANLEY:	Well, why did they ask you to do it?
CLIVE:	It was more me did the asking. Anyway, it was two free tickets.
STANLEY:	What for?
CLIVE:	A play. 30
STANLEY:	(*aloofly*): Was it any good?
CLIVE:	Yes . . . It was splendid, as a matter of fact.
LOUISE:	What was it, dear?
CLIVE:	*Electra*.
STANLEY:	What's that? 35
LOUISE:	(*with exaggerated surprise*): You can't mean it! You just can't mean it.
STANLEY:	Mean what?
LOUISE:	Really, Stanley, there are times when I have to remind myself about you—actually remind myself. 40
STANLEY:	(*quietly*): Suppose you tell me, then. Go on . . . Educate me.
LOUISE:	(*loftily*): Clive dear, you explain it to your father, will you?

Clive sits eating.

STANLEY:	Well, go on. 45
CLIVE:	(*low*): It's Greek.
STANLEY:	Oh, one of those.
LOUISE:	(*brightly*): Who was in it, dear? Laurence Olivier? I always think he's best for those Greek things, don't you? . . . I'll never forget that wonderful night when they put 50 out his eyes—I could hear that scream for weeks and weeks afterwards, everywhere I went.
STANLEY:	(*to Clive*): And that's supposed to be cultured?
CLIVE:	What?
STANLEY:	People having their eyes put out? 55
LOUISE:	It's not people's eyes, Stanley: it's the *poetry*. Of course I don't expect *you* to understand.
STANLEY:	(*to Clive*): And this is what you want to study at Cambridge, when you get up there next month?
CLIVE:	Yes it is, more or less. 60
STANLEY:	May I ask why?
CLIVE:	Well, poetry's its own reward, actually.
STANLEY:	And this is the most useful thing you can find to do with your time?
CLIVE:	It's not a question of useful. 65

STANLEY:	Isn't it?
CLIVE:	Not really.
STANLEY:	(*staring at him gravely*): You don't seem to realise the the world you're living in, my boy. (*Louise gives Clive the lighted cigarette from her cigarette holder.*) When you 70 finish at this university which your mother insists you're to go to, you'll have to earn your living. I won't always be here to pay for everything, you know. All this culture stuff's very fine for those who can afford it; for the nobs and snobs we're always hearing about from 75 that end of the table . . .(*indicating Louise.*) But look here . . . if you can't stand on your own two feet you don't amount to anything. And not one of that pansy set of spongers you're going around with will ever help you do that. 80
CLIVE:	You know nothing about my friends.
STANLEY:	Oh yes I do. I've seen them, Arty-tarty boys. Going around London, giggling and drinking and talking dirty; wearing Bohemian clothes . . . Who did you go out with last night, for instance? 85
CLIVE:	Chuck.
STANLEY:	Chuck? Oh yes, the fellow that never washes. Sings in cafes and wants to stay in school till he's thirty, living on government grants. Such a dignified way to go on. (*Stanley re-lights his pipe.*)

(a)   What is your opinion of (i) Louise, (ii) Stanley? Refer to evidence in the passage to support these opinions.
(b)   What does Clive feel about his parents?
(c)   What differing attitudes do Louise and Stanley have towards their son?
(d)   Choose *three* stage directions. Explain the contribution each makes to the scene.
(e)   Do you feel sorry for Clive? Why?

2.   Point out the ironic implications in each of the following extracts. The first is from *Emma* by Jane Austen, the second from *The Village Inn* by John Betjeman, and the third is slightly adapted from *A Tale of Two Cities* by Charles Dickens, a novel set in the time of the French Revolution of 1789.

(a)   Human nature is so well disposed towards those who are in interesting situations, that a young person, who either marries or dies, is sure of being kindly spoken of.

(b)   "Ah, more than church or school or hall,
The village inn's the heart of all."
So spake the brewer's P. R. O.,
A man who really ought to know,
For he is paid for saying so. 5
And then he kindly gave to me
A lovely coloured booklet free.
'Twas full of prose that sang the praise
Of coaching inns in Georgian days,

Showing how public-houses are   10
More modern than the motor-car,
More English than the weald or wold
And almost equally as old,
And run for love and not for gold
Until I felt a filthy swine   15
For loathing beer and liking wine,
And rotten to the very core
For thinking village inns a bore,
And village bores more sure to roam
To village inns than stay at home.   20

(c) France rolled with exceeding smoothness down hill, making
paper money and spending it. Under the guidance of her Christian
pastors, she entertained herself, besides, with such humane achieve-
ments as sentencing a youth to have his hands cut off, his tongue torn
out with pincers, and his body burned alive, because he had not 5
kneeled down in the rain to do honour to a dirty procession of monks
which passed within his view, at a distance of some fifty or sixty yards.

VIII FOR DISCUSSION

1. Does nonsense verse *mean* anything? Is there any sense in it? Consider such famous
poems as *Jabberwocky* by Lewis Carroll and *The Dong with the Luminous Nose* by
Edward Lear.

2. Read the following poem:

The Loch Ness Monster's Song

Sssnnnwhuffffll?
Hnwhuffl hhnnwfl hnfl hfl?
Gdroblboblhobngbl gbl gl g g g g glbgl.
Drublhaflablhaflubhafgabhaflhafl fl fl—
gm grawwwww grf grawf awfgm graw gm.   5
Hovoplodok-doplodovok-plovodokot-doplodokosh?
Splgraw fok fok splgrafhatchgabrlgabrl fok splfok!
Zgra kra gka fok!
Grof grawff gahf?
Gombl mbl bl—   10
blm plm,
blm plm,
blm plm,
blp.

by Edwin Morgan

This sort of poem is sometimes referred to as *concrete* poetry. Does it have a meaning?
Does it convey anything to you? How important is the title in suggesting to you that it
may be about something? Do different lines suggest different things?

3. Here is another poem by the same author, Edwin Morgan.

The Computer's First Christmas Card

jolly merry
holly berry
jolly berry
merry holly
happy jolly   5
jolly jelly
jelly belly
belly merry
holly happy
jolly Molly   10
merry Jarry
merry Harry
happy Barry
hoppy Jarry
boppy happy   15
barry jarry
jarry jolly
moppy jelly
Molly merry
Jarry jolly   20
belly boppy
jarry hoppy
holly moppy
Barry merry
Jarry happy   25
happy boppy
boppy jolly
jolly merry
merry merry
merry merry   30
merry Chris
amerryasa
Chrisamerry
asmerrychrr
YSANTHEMUM   35

Does this poem make any serious points or criticism about computers? What do you notice about the word pattern of the poem? Can you explain in what ways concrete poetry differs from the more traditional forms of verse?

IX   FOR FURTHER READING
Marjorie Boulton **The Anatomy of Language** *(Routledge & Kegan Paul)*
John F. Danby **Approach to Poetry** *(Heinemann)*
Ted Hughes **Poetry in the Making** *(Faber)*

X   MORE ADVANCED READING
Robert Millar & Ian Currie **The Language of Prose** *(Heinemann)*
Robert Millar & Ian Currie **The Language of Poetry** *(Heinemann)*
B. A. Phythian **Considering Poetry** *(English Universities Press)*
Alan Warner **A Short Guide to English Style** *(Oxford)*

SIX POEMS

INTRODUCTION

In this section six poems are printed together with summaries and appreciations. These poems are of high quality, are fairly demanding on the reader, and are regularly included among the set texts in the syllabuses of many examinations boards. They are in fact typical of the sort of poetry which is often set and this is a reason for their inclusion here.

There is another reason. Despite the fact that they may have mastered the concepts dealt with in Section A of this book many young people—like yourself and including yourself, perhaps—have difficulty in sustaining at any length their writing about a particular poem; and experience shows that you nearly always profit a great deal if you have a chance to read some models of criticism which are written in a language you can understand.

The phrase "models of criticism" sounds pretentious. There is certainly no claim that the commentaries on the poems which follow say all there is to say or are anything like perfect. If they happen to throw some light on these particular poems, this in itself will be profitable, but they also try to show you a method, a means of approach to a poem, a way of getting started, and so enable you to make valid attempts on your own with poems not discussed here.

A word about the summaries. It is quite impossible to capture entirely a poet's meaning in this way, but the summaries have been found useful by pupils who have confessed to bewilderment after the first few readings of a poem. They are, it is hoped, an aid to understanding.

You should be quite clear in your own mind that before you can attempt to make any appreciative comment or express any valid opinion about a poem, or, indeed, any work of art, you must be able to make some claim to having understood it. Understanding is the first thing to aim for. It is often difficult.

The first poet in this section—Keats—is a good example. When a poet has something unusual, or very personal, or extremely complex to say, he is forced to wrestle with words and with the form in which to say it. In turn you, the reader, will find that you have to struggle with the meaning. You need patience and concentration and determination, because the task is often difficult and time-consuming. You may need to return to a poem again and again over a long period of time to think about it and to revise your thoughts.

Fortunately, in the examples which follow, much of this groundwork has been done for you!

1. **Ode To A Nightingale** *by John Keats*

I   My heart aches, and a drowsy numbness pains
        My sense, as though of hemlock I had drunk
    Or emptied some dull opiate to the drains
        One minute past, and Lethe-wards had sunk:
    'Tis not through envy of thy happy lot,   5
        But being too happy in thine happiness,—
            That thou, light-wingèd Dryad of the trees,
                In some melodious plot
    Of beechen green, and shadows numberless,
        Singest of summer in full-throated ease.   10

II   O, for a draught of vintage! that hath been
        Cool'd a long age in the deep-delvèd earth,
    Tasting of Flora and the country green,
        Dance, and Provençal song, and sunburnt mirth!
    O for a beaker full of the warm South,   15
        Full of the true, the blushful Hippocrene,
            With beaded bubbles winking at the brim,
                And purple-stainèd mouth;
    That I might drink, and leave the world unseen,
        And with thee fade away into the forest dim: 20

III   Fade far away, dissolve, and quite forget
        What thou among the leaves hast never known,
    The weariness, the fever, and the fret
        Here, where men sit and hear each other groan;
    Where palsy shakes a few, sad, last grey hairs,   25
        Where youth grows pale, and spectre-thin, and dies;
            Where but to think is to be full of sorrow
                And leaden-eyed despairs,
    Where Beauty cannot keep her lustrous eyes,
        Or new Love pine at them beyond to-morrow.   30

IV   Away! away! for I will fly to thee,
        Not charioted by Bacchus and his pards,
    But on the viewless wings of Poesy,
        Though the dull brain perplexes and retards:
    Already with thee! tender is the night,   35
        And haply the Queen-Moon is on her throne,
            Cluster'd around by all her starry Fays;
                But here there is no light,
    Save what from heaven is with the breezes blown
        Through verdurous glooms and winding mossy ways.   40

V   I cannot see what flowers are at my feet,
        Nor what soft incense hangs upon the boughs,
    But, in embalmèd darkness, guess each sweet
        Wherewith the seasonable month endows

The grass, the thicket, and the fruit-tree wild;   45
  White hawthorn, and the pastoral eglantine;
    Fast fading violets cover'd up in leaves;
      And mid-May's eldest child,
The coming musk-rose, full of dewy wine,
      The murmurous haunt of flies on summer eves.   50

VI   Darkling I listen; and, for many a time
  I have been half in love with easeful Death,
Call'd him soft names in many a musèd rhyme,
  To take into the air my quiet breath;
Now more than ever seems it rich to die,   55
  To cease upon the midnight with no pain,
    While thou art pouring forth thy soul abroad
      In such an ecstasy!
Still wouldst thou sing, and I have ears in vain—
  To thy high requiem become a sod.   60

VII   Thou wast not born for death, immortal Bird!
  No hungry generations tread thee down;
The voice I hear this passing night was heard
  In ancient days by emperor and clown;
Perhaps the self-same song that found a path   65
  Through the sad heart of Ruth, when, sick for home,
    She stood in tears amid the alien corn;
      The same that oft-times hath
Charm'd magic casements, opening on the foam
  Of perilous seas, in faery lands forlorn.   70

VIII Forlorn! the very word is like a bell
  To toll me back from thee to my sole self!
Adieu! the fancy cannot cheat so well
  As she is fam'd to do, deceiving elf.
Adieu! adieu! thy plaintive anthem fades   75
  Past the near meadows, over the still stream,
    Up the hill-side; and now 'tis buried deep
      In the next valley-glades:
Was it a vision, or a waking dream?
  Fled is that music:—Do I wake or sleep?   80

SUMMARY

Verse 1   The poet describes his physical feelings. His senses are painful and dulled as if he had drunk poison or consumed some sleep-inducing drug. His state of mind is caused not by envy of the nightingale's good fortune but rather because he is overwhelmed by its happy song. The bird sings eagerly of summer in some green wood.

Verse 2   The poet wishes for wine and for poetic inspiration (Hippocrene) so that he might escape from the world and join the nightingale in the forest.

Verse 3   The poet tries to forget what the nightingale in the wood has never known: the miseries that beset mankind. He wants to leave the real world with its pains and torment, illness, death and despair, where all that is beautiful grows old.

Verse 4   He rejects wine as his means of escape. He will rely solely upon poetry despite the difficulties of composition in his present state of mind. In his imagination he joins the nightingale and describes the darkness of the wood in which he finds himself.

Verse 5   The poet cannot see the flowers and plants around him. He guesses their identity by smelling their fragrance.

Verse 6   In the darkness the poet contemplates the peacefulness of death as a means of escape. At this moment, while the nightingale is singing, death without pain would be a luxury. The nightingale would continue to sing, although the poet, being dead, would be deaf to its song.

Verse 7   The song of the nightingale has been heard at different times in different circumstances by different people through the centuries. In this sense it is immortal. The song is not part of the misery of human existence: it belongs to the world of faery.

Verse 8   The word "forlorn" recalls the poet from his deep contemplation of the nightingale's song. He realises that his poetic imagination may create illusions but it cannot sustain them, as is commonly supposed, and so this flight of his imagination is simply deceptive. The poet therefore bids farewell to the nightingale as its song fades across the countryside. He is left perplexed and wondering about the source of his inspiration.

APPRECIATION

The *Ode to a Nightingale* is generally regarded as one of the best, if not the most perfect, of Keats's poems. It considers the nature of life and contemplates death as a means of escape from the troubles and anguish of the world.

The first verse opens with the description of a sense of pain (*aches, drowsy numbness pains/My sense*) mingled with a feeling of lethargy, of a drugged sleep, leading to forgetfulness. The verse moves slowly, even sluggishly, with heavy stresses at the end of the second and fourth lines and long drawn-out rhymes in lines 1 and 3. The punctuation adds to this with a long pause after only three words and a further pause near the beginning of line 2. It is as if the verse were having difficulty getting going, the enjambement of line 3 unable to be sustained beyond four syllables before a further downward movement suggestive of tiredness and despair (*Lethe-wards had sunk*). A lighter tone is revealed by lines 5, 6 and 7, when the nightingale is introduced, and, with the aid of the short eighth line, the verse moves more swiftly to a close with a pleasing picture of summer greenery, shadows and bird-song.

The first verse introduces two major ideas upon which the poem is built: Keats's mood and the song of the nightingale. The second verse, in praise of the qualities of wine, is one of sensuous pleasure. The coolness of the wine (line 12) contrasts with the warmth, happiness, movement and flowers of summer. Typical of Keats is his use of hyphenated words (*deep-delvèd*, *purple-stainèd*), his recording of carefully observed detail (*beaded bubbles winking at the brim*), and a sureness of touch, which is revealed by his use of an apt adjective or evocative phrase (*sunburnt mirth, the warm South, blushful*). The repeated *O* suggests a real longing. This repetition also provides the structural framework of the stanza: it is not until we reach lines 19 and 20 that we realise that the desire for wine is related to the wish to escape with the nightingale. Lines 11 to 18 elaborately describe the qualities of wine. Lines 19 and 20 reveal the purpose of the wine-drinking: to *fade away into the forest* with the nightingale. The darkness of the forest is emphasised by the placing of the adjective *dim* after its noun and as the last word in this verse.

Notice that the whole of stanzas 2 and 3 is one long sentence. Lines 19 and 20, within this sentence, introduce the idea of escape from the human sufferings that are listed in the third verse. The sense spills over from one stanza to the next, *with thee fade away* being taken up in *Fade far away* at the start of the third verse.

In this third verse Keats's desire to forget what the nightingale has never known causes him in fact to remember things of a particularly painful kind. The whole stanza is remarkable for its force of description and its precise use of words: *dissolve, groan, spectre-thin, leaden-eyed, pine*. The suffering and anguish of mankind is dwelt on by collecting together powerful nouns (*weariness, fever, fret*), by the use of four stark adjectives in an image of age and disease (*palsy shakes a few, sad, last grey hairs*), and by the image of youth growing pale through illness and dying. The placing of *Here* at the start of line 24 is sudden and dramatic and shapes the thought of the rest of the stanza by enabling Keats to mount a series of parallel constructions which reveal the transient nature of all things: *Here, where men sit—Where palsy shakes—Where youth grows pale—Where but to think—Where Beauty cannot keep—*

With a repeated exclamation (*Away! away!*) Keats dismisses the dark thoughts of the preceding verse and expresses his wish to join the nightingale, free from the troubles of the world. This fourth stanza is, perhaps, the weakest of the poem. In a rather exaggerated and overdone image (*Not charioted by Bacchus and his pards*) he rejects wine as his means of escape from the world and declares his faith in the imaginative power of poetry. Even so, the image of the Queen-Moon seems rather contrived. Yet the idea of moonlight being blown by the wind through the wood is interesting, and the last line (line 40) has an appropriately solemn atmosphere. Structurally, this stanza, together with stanza 5, serves mainly as a transition between the opening statement of the first three verses and the last three verses of the poem.

In verse 3 the problem of human suffering is clearly recognised; in verse 6 *easeful Death* resolves this problem. The fifth verse, being simply descriptive, does not advance the thought of the poem. There is a richness and profusion of flowers and vegetation, giving off a heavy scent (*incense, embalmèd*), and worthy of note once again is the carefully observed detail of lines 49 and 50 with their sensuous appeals to taste (*dewy wine*) and hearing (*murmurous*). Verse 5 sets the scene for the contemplative thought of the next two verses.

Verse 6, the heart of the poem, exhibits a remarkable intensity of feeling about death. Both in diction and rhythm the first four lines (lines 51-4) are quiet and peaceful and reflect the poet's thoughtful state of mind. Death is personified almost as a lover (*Call'd him soft names*)—though the poet tentatively says that he is only *half in love* with him—and is *easeful*, involving no pain, simply a dissolving of the body into the air. As such, as a release from the tensions and burdens of the world outlined earlier in the poem, it is to be welcomed. In line 55 the tone grows more emphatic: *Now more than ever seems it rich to die*. The nightingale's singing (*pouring forth thy soul*) and the act of dying (*seems it rich to die*) are identified as complementary states of ecstasy. Death at such a moment, when the listener is captivated by the bird's beautiful song, would be a luxury, the song correspondingly becoming a requiem.

These thoughts of death lead naturally to the next sequence, where the idea is expressed in lines 61-2 that the bird's song will live for ever because it is untainted by human woes. *No hungry generations tread thee down* suggests images of conflict and struggle, of which the nightingale is happily unaware. The song is *the self-same* not only through the ages but also in the world of faery. It is unchanging and immortal. And yet, by means of the poem itself, the poet is beginning to change his attitude to the song. Keats speaks of the bird's immortality (*Thou wast not born for death, immortal Bird!*) but through the developing diction of stanza 7—*sad heart, sick for home, in tears, forlorn*—the nightingale's song serves only to remind him of the misery he would prefer to forget.

The bird's song, no longer *an ecstasy*, thus becomes the *plaintive anthem* of stanza 8, where Keats recognises that his art has deceived him and he is brought back to his *sole self* by the echoes of loneliness and desolation in the word *forlorn*. That mood of deeply contemplative concentration, essential to the creation of all great art, is broken by the use of the word *forlorn*, with its echoes of the real world of suffering. In other words, the mood is broken by the very act of writing which was itself responsible for the creation of that mood in the first place (*I will fly to thee . . . on the viewless wings of Poesy*) and the poet is left perplexed and wondering about the significance of his *vision* and its effect on him.

Keats does not mistake his dreams for reality. He ponders deeply on the song of the nightingale and it is through his contemplation of the song that his thoughts on the nature of life and death are conveyed to the reader in a vivid way. Additionally, the poem possesses a spontaneous, living quality. It is as if Keats were living out the experience in words. The poem may be said, in a sense, to be a working example of Keats's belief, which he expressed in a letter to Hessey (9 October 1818), that "That which is creative must create itself." In creating the *Ode to a Nightingale* Keats created one of the great poems of the nineteenth century and one for which he is justly remembered.

2. **Spring Offensive** *by Wilfred Owen*

I
Halted against the shade of a last hill,
They fed, and lying easy, were at ease
And, finding comfortable chests and knees,
Carelessly slept. But many there stood still
To face the stark, blank sky beyond the ridge,   5
Knowing their feet had come to the end of the world.

II
Marvelling they stood, and watched the long grass swirled
By the May breeze, murmurous with wasp and midge,
For though the summer oozed into their veins
Like an injected drug for their bodies' pains,   10
Sharp on their souls hung the imminent line of grass,
Fearfully flashed the sky's mysterious glass.

III
Hour after hour they ponder the warm field—
And the far valley behind, where the buttercup
Had blessed with gold their slow boots coming up,   15
Where even the little brambles would not yield,
But clutched and clung to them like sorrowing hands;
They breathe like trees unstirred.

IV
Till like a cold gust thrills the little word
At which each body and its soul begird   20
And tighten them for battle. No alarms
Of bugles, no high flags, no clamorous haste—
Only a lift and flare of eyes that faced
The sun, like a friend with whom their love is done.
O larger shone that smile against the sun,—   25
Mightier than his whose bounty these have spurned.

V
So, soon they topped the hill, and raced together
Over an open stretch of herb and heather
Exposed. And instantly the whole sky burned
With fury against them; earth set sudden cups   30
In thousands for their blood; and the green slope
Chasmed and steepened sheer to infinite space.

VI
Of them who running on that last high place
Leapt to swift unseen bullets, or went up
On the hot blast and fury of hell's upsurge,   35
Or plunged and fell away past this world's verge,
Some say God caught them even before they fell.
But what say such as from existence' brink
Ventured but drove too swift to sink,
The few who rushed in the body to enter hell,   40
And there out-fiending all its fiends and flames
With superhuman inhumanities,
Long-famous glories, immemorial shames—
And crawling slowly back, have by degrees
Regained cool peaceful air in wonder—   45
Why speak not they of comrades that went under?

SUMMARY

Verse 1   The soldiers rest in the shade of a hill. Some sleep. Many feel apprehensive at what awaits them beyond the ridge.

Verse 2   They wonder at the sights of early summer and yet, though such sights soothe their pains, they cannot dismiss their fear of the danger lurking over the horizon.

Verse 3   Time passes and they look at the field and the valley and its brambles through which they have come. Now the soldiers stand as still as trees undisturbed by the wind.

Verse 4   A warning is given for them to get ready for battle. They prepare quietly and without display.

Verse 5   They reach the top of the hill and charge over the open ground. At once the enemy bombardment begins.

Verse 6   Some people say that those who were killed in the battle are now with God in heaven. But the soldiers who survived, having been involved in all the hellish atrocities of war, when they have reached a place of refuge, say nothing about their comrades who were killed. Why?

APPRECIATION

The poem's dramatic impact results largely from the contrast between Owen's pleasant, summery description of the scene and the unnatural eruption of the landscape as soon as the battle starts.

There is an air of peace and comfort in the first verse (*fed, lying easy, at ease, carelessly slept*) but even here there is a hint of danger: the sky is *stark* and *blank*, impassive, giving nothing away. The men are apprehensive: *Knowing their feet had come to the end of the world*. Owen writes *their feet* as if to suggest that the men themselves would not have come here if they had had any choice. *The end of the world* is explicit enough.

The second and third verses contain some pleasing description of summer and the landscape. The soldiers have time to enjoy the summer atmosphere (*hour after hour*) after their painful, reluctant exertions (*slow boots coming up*). The setting is romantic: *long grass swirled, May breeze, warm field, little brambles*. Yet, though the buttercup *blessed with gold their slow boots*, the landscape vaguely threatens. The grassy horizon is *imminent*, the sky *mysterious*—it now flashes fearfully as if to signal danger—and the brambles *clutched and clung to them like sorrowing hands*, like the hands of relatives, perhaps, or as if they were aware of what was about to happen and did not want the soldiers to go on. The simile, *like trees unstirred*, in the last line of the third verse, identifies the soldiers more closely with the natural landscape and brings the opening movement of the poem to a close.

There is now a transition in the poem's narrative as the soldiers prepare at the word of warning to get ready. *Like a cold gust* continues the image of the *May breeze* and the trees *unstirred* by the wind. *Thrills* is exactly right in describing a sudden chill of fear. The reference to *each body and its soul* makes the reader aware of the tremendous life-and-death issue which is horrifyingly illustrated by the later events in the poem. In contrast the soldiers' preparations are undramatic and barely noticeable. Their only sign of nerves is the recognition in their eyes that this is the moment they have been waiting for.

The tempo of the poem changes in verse 5. The quick, mainly monosyllabic words of the first two lines suggest the speed of the charge, but the word *Exposed*, in its emphatic position at the beginning of the third line and yet right next to a full stop, acts like a sharp cry of warning. The reader is expecting the sentence to continue, to maintain its momentum. The fact that it doesn't, that it suddenly ends on the word *Exposed*, jolts the reader into an awareness of the terrible situation in which the soldiers find themselves. Here now begins the real *Spring Offensive* of the title of the poem. It proves to be a bitterly ironic title, for not only are the soldiers making an attack, an *offensive*, in May (Spring), but it seems as if Nature itself (Spring) is making its own attack upon them, such is the devastation wrought by the bullets and bombs of the enemy. The sky *burned/With fury*, the thousands of holes blasted out of the earth become cups to collect their blood, the *green slope* tips them into the void.

The battle is *hell's upsurge*. The diction is suitably violent: *blast, fury, plunged, rushed in the body to enter hell, fiends and flames*. And there is further bitter irony in the uncertainty of the phrase *Some say God caught them* and in Owen's belief that glorious deeds of battle are in fact *inhumanities*. The inconclusiveness of the ending illustrates the bewildering effect that war has on the minds of the soldiers who survive.

3. Insensibility *by Wilfred Owen*

I   Happy are men who yet before they are killed
        Can let their veins run cold.
        Whom no compassion fleers
        Or makes their feet
        Sore on the alleys cobbled with their brothers.   5
        The front line withers,
        But they are troops who fade, not flowers
        For poets' tearful fooling:
        Men, gaps for filling:
        Losses, who might have fought   10
        Longer; but no one bothers.

II   And some cease feeling
        Even themselves or for themselves.
        Dullness best solves
        The tease and doubt of shelling,   15
        And Chance's strange arithmetic
        Comes simpler than the reckoning of their shilling.
        They keep no check on armies' decimation.

III   Happy are these who lose imagination:
        They have enough to carry with ammunition.   20
        Their spirit drags no pack,
        Their old wounds, save with cold, can not more ache.
        Having seen all things red,
        Their eyes are rid
        Of the hurt of the colour of blood for ever.   25
        And terror's first constriction over,
        Their hearts remain small-drawn.
        Their senses in some scorching cautery of battle
        Now long since ironed,
        Can laugh among the dying, unconcerned.   30

IV   Happy the soldier home, with not a notion
        How somewhere, every dawn, some men attack,
        And many sighs are drained.
        Happy the lad whose mind was never trained:
        His days are worth forgetting more than not.   35
        He sings along the march
        Which we march taciturn, because of dusk,
        The long, forlorn, relentless trend
        From larger day to huger night.

V   We wise, who with a thought besmirch   40
        Blood over all our soul,
        How should we see our task
        But through his blunt and lashless eyes?
        Alive, he is not vital overmuch;

Dying, not mortal overmuch;   45
Nor sad, nor proud,
Nor curious at all.
He cannot tell
Old men's placidity from his.

VI   But cursed are dullards whom no cannon stuns,   50
That they should be as stones;
Wretched are they, and mean
With paucity that never was simplicity.
By choice they made themselves immune
To pity and whatever mourns in man   55
Before the last sea and the hapless stars;
Whatever mourns when many leave these shores;
Whatever shares
The eternal reciprocity of tears.

SUMMARY

Verse 1.   Soldiers who can condition themselves to be devoid of physical and mental feeling before they are killed in battle are described ironically as *happy*. All soldiers are expendable, and it is foolish for poets to mourn for them. Troops are merely men who fight, and no one bothers about what happens to them.

Verse 2.   They take refuge from the fear and uncertainty of their fate on the battle-field in a dullness which numbs their senses. They keep no account of the destruction of armies.

Verse 3.   Their finer feelings are blunted by routine, by personal discomfort and pain, by the familiar sight of blood and the terror of war, so that they become callous and uncaring.

Verse 4.   The soldier at home can be described as *happy* because he has no idea of the battles and deaths that are occurring elsewhere. The young man who has never yet known war can also be described as *happy*. He sings as he marches, in contrast to those who have been at the battle-front. They are silent. For them dusk only brings, as always, the even greater burden of night-time to add to that of the day.

Verse 5.   These soldiers are *wise* because they know the horror of war, unlike the inexperienced soldier who lacks their perception of what war entails. They recognise that his life, or death, is of little significance. The inexperienced soldier does not understand that the calmness of these old warriors, stemming from callousness, is different from the calmness of his own untroubled disposition.

Verse 6.   The poet denounces those civilians who are heartlessly insensitive to the plight of the soldiers. These civilians are all the more wretched because their meanness of spirit does not arise from lack of knowledge or judgement. They have deliberately crushed within themselves all sense of pity, so that they are unaffected by sorrow or by those feelings of mutual sympathy and understanding which have lasted for all time.

APPRECIATION

The poem examines two aspects of "insensibility" (or indifference) as it occurs first of all in the soldiers and secondly in civilians.

There are many points worthy of comment in the poem. It opens with a startling and ironic statement that men who are about to be killed are *happy* if they can make themselves indifferent to the fate of others, and the word "happy" becomes the point of return in succeeding stanzas (III and IV) and serves as the point of departure in the contrasting idea of *cursed* in the last stanza (VI). The factual phrase *before they are killed* suggests that there is no escape, that slaughter is inevitable, and that such slaughter is in no way out of the ordinary or upsetting. *Fleers* is an unusual word. It means "to laugh in derision at". It has an unpleasant, mocking ring like the word "jeer" or "sneer". The image of the dead serving as cobble-stones brings out the "insensibility" that is the theme of the poem, as does the flower image in lines 6-8. The use of a dying flower as an image of sadness and loss is a familiar one in literature. Here the poet ironically reverses the idea: the soldiers are not as important as the flowers that poets write silly poems about: they are *gaps for filling*, merely *Losses*. The alliteration of 'l' and 'f' in these lines (6-11) is particularly clever and aids the rhythmical impetus of the verse as one idea succeeds another.

Chance's strange arithmetic in verse 2 conveys the idea that being killed in war is merely a statistical event, calling for no emotional response. The horror of it is deliberately played down. It *comes simpler* than adding up the shillings the soldiers used to be paid for enlisting. In other words, death is everywhere but it is not a matter of real concern.

Verse 3 helps to explain why. The central idea of the poem is that

> *Having seen all things red,*
> *Their eyes are rid*
> *Of the hurt of the colour of blood for ever.*

Here Owen does not blame the soldiers for their "insensible" attitude. He understands that their lack of feeling, their loss of *imagination*, has been caused by the horrors they have been through. War has seared their senses like a branding iron. It is not their fault if they have been made callous. It is their only means of defence against being overwhelmed by fear:

> *Dullness best solves*
> *The tease and doubt of shelling.*

To be compassionate in such a situation is to risk being driven mad.

The fourth verse turns attention to the soldier at home and to the youth who has not yet fought in battle. There is little to comment on in this verse. The contrasting of his lack of experience with that of the older soldiers — expressed in his singing — is an obvious one. It develops the theme of the poem in a functional, but unoriginal, way.

The fifth verse reveals the thought of the soldiers who are steeped in war. The cynicism of *We wise* is disturbing. Life or death arouses no human feeling in them, and they dismiss the youth's inexperience as ignorance:

> *He cannot tell*
> *Old men's placidity from his.*

And yet Owen does not condemn them. His condemnation is reserved for the civilians *whom no cannon stuns* in the last verse. The poet protests strongly against them for having *by choice* made themselves indifferent to the fate of soldiers on the battle-field. He recognises that soldiers can become "insensible" and lack all compassion, but he understands that this is a horrific consequence of war. The civilian *dullards*, however, have no excuse for their attitude, and so they are *cursed* and degenerate, the target of Owen's scorn.

The poem ends with images which seek to establish the value of pity and the eternal relevance of such human feeling.

4.   The Unknown Citizen *by W. H. Auden*

(To JS/07/M/378
This Marble Monument
Is erected by the State)

He was found by the Bureau of Statistics to be
One against whom there was no official complaint,
And all the reports on his conduct agree
That, in the modern sense of an old-fashioned word, he was a saint,
For in everything he did he served the Greater Community.   5
Except for the War till the day he retired
He worked in a factory and never got fired,
But satisfied his employers, Fudge Motors Inc.
Yet he wasn't a scab or odd in his views,
For his Union reports that he paid his dues,   10
(Our report on his Union shows it was sound)
And our Social Psychology workers found
That he was popular with his mates and liked a drink.
The Press are convinced that he bought a paper every day
And that his reactions to advertisements were normal in every way.   15
Policies taken out in his name prove that he was fully insured,
And his Health-card shows he was once in hospital but left it cured.
Both Producers Research and High-Grade Living declare
He was fully sensible to the advantages of the Instalment Plan
And had everything necessary to the Modern Man,   20
A phonograph, a radio, a car and a frigidaire.
Our researchers into Public Opinion are content
That he held the proper opinions for the time of year;
When there was peace, he was for peace; when there was war, he
      went.
He was married and added five children to the population,   25
Which our Eugenist says was the right number for a parent of his
      generation,
And our teachers report that he never interfered with their education.
Was he free? Was he happy? The question is absurd:
Had anything been wrong, we should certainly have heard.

APPRECIATION

This poem is an ironic comment on the standardised pattern of modern society and modern living. As can be seen in the dedication (*To JS/07/M/378*), the Unknown Citizen is just a number, a nameless face among the millions. This negative quality is established in the first two lines of the poem:

> *He was found by the Bureau of Statistics to be*
> *One against whom there was no official complaint.*

In an inscription on a marble monument one would expect to find evidence of high human merit, of deèds and qualities of distinction, but nothing positive emerges here: the praise of the Unknown Citizen is given solely because there was no official complaint made against him. If this is a virtue, there is at least the implication that it is a virtue not shared by thousands of his fellow men, that there was much official complaining to be made about their conduct; so that, whatever way the lines are read, a critical point is made: either to recognise the undesirable conduct of society generally, or to recognise the specious nature of the praise bestowed upon the Unknown Citizen by the State.

If the praise is hollow, it matches the life of the Unkown Citizen. *He never got fired.* He *wasn't a scab or odd in his views.* He held *the proper opinions for the time of year.* He never interfered with education. The Social Psychology workers discovered nothing to establish him as an individual: *he was popular with his mates and liked a drink.*

The discoveries of the Press, similarly, find nothing which will distinguish him from the mass of people. Their conviction that he bought a paper every day tries to make a trivial act sound grandly important, but only shows the superficiality of his life. Of his private life nothing is learned beyond the stark facts that he was fully insured and had been in hospital; nothing about the values he held, or about his dreams, ambitions, kindnesses, love for his children, only that he had five, which was *the right number* according to the population expert. Yet he had everything necessary to the modern man:

> *A phonograph, a radio, a car and a frigidaire—*

everything material, that is, and all on hire purchase *(the Instalment Plan).*

> *When there was peace, he was for peace; when there was war, he went.*

He went along with the crowd. He reflects its life and its views. He *is* the crowd with its humdrum living and distorted emphasis on material possessions. This, says Auden, is what modern society is like. We conform to a standard pattern without ever asking the basic questions:

> *Was he free? Was he happy? The question is absurd:*
> *Had anything been wrong, we should certainly have heard.*

The proof of our conformity, of the shallowness of our existence, lies in the fact that if we did not find comfort in this way of life and the things that go with it, we would have done something about it. We would have complained: the State would have heard about it. The life of the Unknown Citizen is like the life of everybody else. He is unidentifiable because he is precisely the same as everybody else.

5. **An Arundel Tomb** *by Philip Larkin*

I   Side by side, their faces blurred,
The earl and countess lie in stone,
Their proper habits vaguely shown
As jointed armour, stiffened pleat,
And that faint hint of the absurd—   5
The little dogs under their feet.

II   Such plainness of the pre-baroque
Hardly involves the eye, until
It meets his left-hand gauntlet, still
Clasped empty in the other; and   10
One sees, with a sharp tender shock,
His hand withdrawn, holding her hand.

III   They would not think to lie so long.
Such faithfulness in effigy
Was just a detail friends would see: 15
A sculptor's sweet commissioned grace
Thrown off in helping to prolong
The Latin names around the base.

IV   They would not guess how early in
Their supine stationary voyage   20
The air would change to soundless damage,
Turn the old tenantry away;
How soon succeeding eyes begin
To look, not read. Rigidly they

V   Persisted, linked through lengths and breadths   25
Of time. Snow fell, undated. Light
Each summer thronged the glass. A bright
Litter of birdcalls strewed the same
Bone-riddled ground. And up the paths
The endless altered people came,   30

VI   Washing at their identity.
Now, helpless in the hollow of
An unarmorial age, a trough
Of smoke in slow suspended skeins
Above their scrap of history,   35
Only an attitude remains:

VII   Time has transfigured them into
Untruth. The stone fidelity
They hardly meant has come to be
Their final blazon, and to prove   40
Our almost-instinct almost true:
What will survive of us is love.

SUMMARY

Verse 1. The poet sees the figures of the earl and his wife carved on the top of the stone tomb. Their features have worn away. He describes their clothes and the pet dogs that lie at their feet.

Verse 2. The plain, unelaborate carving creates little interest for an observer but suddenly the onlooker is surprised to see that the couple are holding hands.

Verse 3. This small, symbolic act of their faithfulness to each other would be seen by their friends but would generally pass unnoticed. It would be little more than a kind after-thought added by the sculptor who had been paid to carve the statues.

Verse 4. The earl and countess would not have guessed how soon the passing of time would alter things: make the stone crumble, move people away from the land, reduce Latin to a dead language.

Verse 5. The couple have remained, holding hands, through time. Throughout the ages different visitors have come to see the tomb.

Verse 6. The present age is unheraldic and does not understand the past. All that remains is the pose of the stone figures and the feelings suggested by that posture.

Verse 7. The holding of hands is an image of faithfulness, but, since such faithfulness was not really intended by the earl and countess, this idea is not really truthful. Nevertheless it has come through time to be the final record of their virtue, and so the poet concludes by saying that love will survive us, or, rather, he somewhat inconclusively states that it is *almost* true to say that what will survive of us will be love.

APPRECIATION

Philip Larkin had in mind, when writing this poem, a particular tomb in the grounds of Chichester Cathedral. It is one of his best poems, possessing those qualities of elegance and control for which Larkin is famous.

The poem begins with a description of the earl and countess, whose effigies are carved on the lid of the tomb. Their faces are *blurred* because over the years the stone has been worn away. At first there appears to be nothing unusual about these figures, but in the second verse the onlooker is surprised to see that they are holding hands. This verse is remarkable for the poet's compression of language and for the impersonal tone (*One sees*), a note which is sustained throughout the poem. The sense of surprise is accurately described (*sharp tender shock*).

Verse 3 opens with a somewhat wistful statement: *They would not think to lie so long.* In this verse, and in succeeding verses, the poet reflects upon the significance of the stone figures. The word *lie* in line 13 is linked with the same word in line 2 of the poem and also with the word *Untruth* in line 38. The word is used in a double sense: that of physically lying down (as the statues are lying on the top of the tomb) and also in the sense of not telling the truth, of being deliberately misleading (and in a sense the *message* that the statues have for us today is misleading, since it was not intended by the sculptor and has been distorted by time). *Faithfulness* in line 14 also has a double meaning: that of being faithful in love and that of a likeness, a similarity between the real-life earl and countess and the figures of the sculpture. Larkin suggests that the sculptor's manufacture of the detail of the earl and countess holding hands is a trifle (*Thrown off*) which the sculptor added as an after-thought. It was the sort of compliment for which he was paid (*commissioned*) in any case.

In verse 4 the oxymoron *stationary voyage* describes perfectly the journey which the effigies have made through space and time, lying flat on their backs (*supine*) as one might imagine spacemen making such a journey. *Soundless damage* suggests quiet but inevitable decay, and the adverb *Rigidly* in line 24 is particularly appropriate. The figures are rigid because they are made of stone and are inflexible, but the word also describes their determination, their perseverance in making their journey.

Verse 5 presents a series of images to describe the passing of time:

> Snow fell, undated. Light
> Each summer thronged the glass. A bright
> Litter of birdcalls strewed the same
> Bone-riddled ground.

The reference here is to particular aspects of the seasons of winter (*Snow*) and summer (*Light*), and so the passing of time is more easy to visualise because the poet is not talking in abstractions such as "Time passes". The word *undated* suggests an enormous span of time because the seasonal event—the falling of snow—cannot be placed with any accuracy. *Thronged* suggests the effect the sunlight has on the stained-glass windows, making them seem alive and full of people. The reference to death (the *Bone-riddled ground* of the graveyard) is a timely and serious reminder of the mortality of human beings.

Verses 6 and 7 draw together the threads of the poet's reflections on the tomb. The passing of time has endowed the statues of the earl and countess with a significance which was not there originally. *Only an attitude remains,* says the poet; but it is this attitude, this positioning of the stone in the holding of hands, which carries all the meaning for modern times. In the word *scrap* there may be a suggestion, perhaps, of an historical scrap-book, but its main effect is to belittle the statues. This is reinforced by the adjective "stone" in *stone fidelity*. It suggests hardness and coldness both with regard to the figures themselves and to their attitude to each other in real life. Despite the fact that the statues are holding hands there is no evidence to suggest that the earl and countess really loved each other. (*The stone fidelity/They hardly meant . . .*)

And yet the last line of the poem seems to make a positive and moral statement. *What will survive of us is love.* Its meaning is, however, very subtly qualified by the penultimate line. No great claim is made for love: it is an *almost-instinct* rather than any grand or lasting passion or force for good, and it is only *almost true* that *What will survive of us is love.* And so the poem ends not so much with a moral truth as with a statement which is gently ironic, mocking and detached from human feelings. *What will survive of us is love* turns out to be only partly true. It is a realistic rather than a sentimental view. As in so many of his poems, Larkin observes and records dispassionately and, though he mentions *us* and although he has some sympathy for the human condition, he himself does not feel totally involved.

6. The Whitsun Weddings *by Philip Larkin*

I   That Whitsun, I was late getting away:
      Not till about
One-twenty on the sunlit Saturday
Did my three-quarters-empty train pull out,
All windows down, all cushions hot, all sense   5
Of being in a hurry gone. We ran
Behind the backs of houses, crossed a street
Of blinding windscreens, smelt the fish-dock; thence
The river's level drifting breadth began,
Where sky and Lincolnshire and water meet.   10

II   All afternoon, through the tall heat that slept
      For miles inland,
A slow and stopping curve southwards we kept.
Wide farms went by, short-shadowed cattle, and
Canals with floatings of industrial froth;   15
A hothouse flashed uniquely: hedges dipped
And rose: and now and then a smell of grass
Displaced the reek of buttoned carriage-cloth
Until the next town, new and nondescript,
Approached with acres of dismantled cars.   20

III   At first, I didn't notice what a noise
      The weddings made
Each station that we stopped at: sun destroys
The interest of what's happening in the shade,
And down the long cool platforms whoops and skirls   25
I took for porters larking with the mails,
And went on reading. Once we started, though,
We passed them, grinning and pomaded, girls
In parodies of fashion, heels and veils,
All posed irresolutely, watching us go,   30

IV   As if out on the end of an event
      Waving goodbye
To something that survived it. Struck, I leant
More promptly out next time, more curiously,
And saw it all again in different terms: 35
The fathers with broad belts under their suits
And seamy foreheads; mothers loud and fat;
An uncle shouting smut; and then the perms,
The nylon gloves and jewellery-substitutes,
The lemons, mauves, and olive-ochres that   40

V   Marked off the girls unreally from the rest.
         Yes, from cafés
And banquet-halls up yards, and bunting-dressed
Coach-party annexes, the wedding-days
Were coming to an end. All down the line   45
Fresh couples climbed aboard: the rest stood round;
The last confetti and advice were thrown,
And, as we moved, each face seemed to define
Just what it saw departing: children frowned
At something dull; fathers had never known   50

VI   Success so huge and wholly farcical;
         The women shared
The secret like a happy funeral;
While girls, gripping their handbags tighter, stared
At a religious wounding. Free at last,   55
And loaded with the sum of all they saw,
We hurried towards London, shuffling gouts of steam.
Now fields were building-plots, and poplars cast
Long shadows over major roads, and for
Some fifty minutes, that in time would seem   60

VII   Just long enough to settle hats and say
         I nearly died,
A dozen marriages got under way.
They watched the landscape, sitting side by side
—An Odeon went past, a cooling tower,   65
And someone running up to bowl—and none
Thought of the others they would never meet
Or how their lives would all contain this hour.
I thought of London spread out in the sun,
Its postal districts packed like squares of wheat: 70

VIII   There we were aimed. And as we raced across
         Bright knots of rail
Past standing Pullmans, walls of blackened moss
Came close, and it was nearly done, this frail
Travelling coincidence; and what it held   75
Stood ready to be loosed with all the power
That being changed can give. We slowed again,
And as the tightened brakes took hold, there swelled
A sense of falling, like an arrow-shower
Sent out of sight, somewhere becoming rain.   80

SUMMARY

Verse 1.   The poet sets the scene at the start of a train journey (from Hull to London).

Verse 2.   The journey southwards is described.

Verse 3.   At first the poet doesn't notice the wedding parties at each station. He is reading and assumes that their noise (*whoops and skirls*) is made by porters loading and unloading the mail, but when the train starts again the poet sees the wedding parties on the platform.

Verse 4.   Intrigued by this sight, the poet takes more notice at the next station, where again a wedding party is bidding farewell to a newly married couple. The fathers, mothers, a particular uncle, and the gaudy costumes of the girls catch his eye.

Verse 5.   Similar events have happened at every station. The reactions of the people in the wedding parties are described in this verse and the next one. Children are bored, fathers . . .

Verse 6.   are cynical; women are tearful; young girls intensely interested by the religious ceremonial and sexual aspects of marriage (*religious wounding*). The train now moves non-stop towards London.

Verse 7.   The newly married couples settle themselves on the train. They talk of the events of the day and watch the landscape, thinking only of themselves. They do not think of the other couples, nor do they think of how their marriage (*this hour*) will affect the rest of their lives. The poet turns his attention, somewhat non-committally, to London.

Verse 8.   The train nears London, travelling at speed past standing coaches and through tunnels. The passengers prepare to disembark. The train slows. The poet brings his poem to a close by the use of an image which suggests mixed feelings about the eventual fate of the marriages.

APPRECIATION

This poem has been described by Jonathan Raban as "one of the best poems to have been published since the war". It is a good example of Larkin's observation of human individuals and social events, and is chiefly remarkable for its subtle humour and realistic awareness of contemporary life.

The first verse opens conversationally with the phrase *That Whitsun, I was late getting away*. The easy, rhythmic flow of the words in lines 2-6 sets a pattern of movement which is to become characteristic of the whole poem. Larkin picks up only essential details to set the scene (*sunlit*, the hot cushions, *blinding windscreens*, and line 10.)

The second verse describes the passing landscape. The effect is one of langour (*All afternoon, tall heat, slept, slow and stopping*). There is, again, some carefully observed detail (*Canals with floatings of industrial froth*, a *hothouse*, the *smell of grass* and of *carriage-cloth*). Notice the rather depressing image, in lines 19 and 20, of the scrap-yard which heralds the next town on the journey, and the scathing criticism contained in the coupling of the adjectives *new and nondescript*.

The first two verses set the scene. Verse 3 begins to take us into the heart of the poem. The smoothly conversational tone of the poet is particularly apparent in lines 21-23; the statement

> sun destroys
> *The interest of what's happening in the shade*

is an accurate observation; in line 25 the images appeal both to the sense of touch and of hearing. The words *grinning and pomaded*, supported by *parodies*, reveal the poet's critical attitude to the girls in the wedding party. He is curious to see the same thing at the next station, and is not, perhaps, as detached in his description of what he sees, as he is in some of his other poems. Some people have found the description of the fathers, mothers, and the uncle and the gaudy clothes slightly patronising; and certainly Larkin is sensitive to the vulgar detail (the *broad belts*, the *seamy foreheads*, the simple, unglamorous description of the mothers—note the emphatic inversion of the natural word order here—the dirty-minded uncle, the cheap clothes and the garish colours which make the girls look unreal) but perhaps this may be taken more as an indication that the poem is about *not* belonging, about watching other people's attempts to obtain enduring love without being directly involved oneself. The people involved in the weddings seem slightly ridiculous to Larkin, and this suggests his inability to enter fully into their happiness rather than active dislike of them.

There is a touch of humour in Larkin's observation. Notice the force of *up yards*, *Coach-party annexes*, *Fresh*, the comic fusion of ideas in *The last confetti and advice were thrown* (an example of zeugma), and *happy funeral*.

In line 55 the poet returns to the journey and to his view of the landscape from the train window. Notice his selection of the expression *I nearly died* to convey so much of what the newly married couples would be talking about. Notice, too, the pun in *got under way*, and the incompleteness of the action in *And someone running up to bowl*, which shows that the train has passed by before the action is finished. A small detail like this suggests the experience is drawn from real life.

The last stanza and a half build the poem to a splendid and serious climax. There is a sense of urgency as the train races across *Bright knots of rail* and the image of the train being directed like an arrow towards London is clearly evident in the words *aimed*, *loosed, arrow-shower, sent*. The image of the arrow-shower can be taken to be a sad one, since rain is often an image of tragedy or sorrow or the mundane, and is associated with tears and despondency, so that the end of the poem may be suggesting that these marriages are doomed to failure. Alternatively, the image could be regarded as a happy one since falling rain makes crops grow, just as the marriages now being celebrated may one day lead to the bearing of children. The more convincing interpretation is probably the former.

INTRODUCTION

In this section there are two prose passages and a poem which are typical of the sort of question set in many 'O' Level, 16+ and CSE examinations.

These passages and the poem are printed together with some answers which were written under examination conditions by pupils of quite high ability.

You will gain a great deal by first of all tackling the questions for yourself *without looking at the given answers*. Only inferior beings cheat, and, since you have always thought of yourself—quite rightly—as being very nearly superhuman, the thought is beneath you. Other, contemptible creatures may look, but not you. Among your many admirable qualities are the sheer willpower to discipline yourself and the commonsense to know that your teacher would know if you cheated anyway.

When your marked answers are returned to you, carefully compare them with the answers which were written in the examination room. Take note of how these answers have been marked, and study the suggestions as to how some of them could have been improved.

In this way you will obtain a clear idea about approaches, standards, and the sort of relevant writing which is accurate and earns marks.

You should then be in a strong position to tackle successfully the final section of this book.

1. *From* **Mr Corbett's Ghost** *by Leon Garfield*

A windy night and the old year dying of an ague. Good riddance! A
bad old year, with a mean spring, a poor summer, a bitter autumn—
and now this cold, shivering ague. No one was sorry to see it go. Even
the clouds, all in black, seemed hurrying to its burial somewhere past
Hampstead.   5

In the apothecary's shop in Gospel Oak, the boy Partridge looked up
through the window to a moon that stared fitfully back through the
reflections of big bellied flasks, beakers and retorts. Very soon now
he'd be off to his friends and his home to drink and cheer the death of
the old year—and pray that the new one would be better. And maybe   10

to slip in a prayer for his master, Mister Corbett, the apothecary himself. Such a prayer!

"May you be like this year that's gone, sir, and take the same shivering ague! For your seasons weren't no better."

He stared at the oak bench that shone with his sweat—and at the great 15 stone mortar and pestle in which his spirit had been ground.

"May you creak and groan like your shop sign in this wild wind, sir."

Now there passed by in the moon-striped street a pair of draper's apprentices. Friends. They grinned and waved as they went, and their lips made: "See you later, Ben!" 20

He waved back. They glanced at one another, looked up and down the street and then came leaping quaintly to the shop where they fattened their noses on the window, making pinkish flowers in the glass.

Benjamin made a face. They made two, very diabolical.

"Can we come in, Ben?" 25

"Yes—for a moment."

Into the strange and gloomy shop they came, with looks of cautious wickedness.

"Make a brew, Ben."

"Make a bubbling charm." 30

Like the forced-up sons of witches, they had begun to caper round the great stone mortar. Glumly, Benjamin looked on, wishing he could oblige them, but not knowing how.

Huge wild shadows leaped among the retorts and crucibles, but they were the only uncanny things about . . . save in the apprentices' 35 minds. Now they began to screech and laugh and caper more crazily than ever, so that their faces seemed to dance in the heavy air like rosy fire-flies.

"Turn him into a worm!"

"Turn him into a snail!" 40

"Turn old Corbett into a beetle, Ben—and step on him!"

"Be quiet!" cried Benjamin of a sudden. "He'll hear!"

The draper's apprentices grew still. The stairs at the back of the shop

creaked. But then, so did every other mortal thing in that blustering
night.   45

"Turn him into a—"

But Benjamin Partridge did not hear what other witchcraft was being
asked of him. His mind was suddenly distracted: partly by listening to
a further creaking of the stairs, and partly by a chill and a darkness—
like a cloud across the moon—that had passed over his heart. He 50
shivered. His two friends stared at him: then to each other. They
shrugged their shoulders.

"Happy New Year, Ben."

Then they left him for the more cheerful street. With their going, the
chill within him grew curiously sharper. His back itched, as if he was 55
being watched. He went to the window and waved his friends on their
way; and in the jars that sat like short fat magistrates on the shelves, no
more than a tiny waving Partridge was reflected. A drab dressed little
soul of a boy seemed to struggle to get out.

Now it was half after seven o'clock. Time to be gone. He pulled his 60
patched grey coat from under the counter and began to put it on.

"Sharp to be off, Master Partridge?"

Slippered Mister Corbett was slunk down his stairs, quiet as a
waistcoated rat. Or had he been on the stairs all the time? Uneasily,
Benjamin wondered what his master had heard. Mister Corbett's lips 65
were pressed tight together. A muscle in his cheek twitched and
jumped; his hands were clenched so fiercely that the blood was fled
from his knuckles as if in dismay. Could he have heard?

"It—it's half after seven, Mister Corbett, sir."

"What's half after seven when there's work to be done?"   70

His unpleasant eyes, swollen by spectacles, stared round the shop.
"There's dust on the bottle-tops, Master Partridge. Would you leave
it so? Polish the bottles before you go."

The apprentice sighed, but did as he was told. And Mister Corbett,
pale of face and round of shoulder, watched him.   75

"Not willingly done, Master Partridge. Too anxious to be out and
wild as a fox."

"It's twenty to eight, Mister Corbett, sir. It's New Year's Eve—"

"What's New Year's Eve when there's work to be done? There's a
smear of grease on the bench."   80

Once more the apprentice sighed, but polished away at the mark that had been left by his own sweat.

"Not willingly done, Master Partridge. Your heart wasn't in it. Still less was your soul. I want your heart and soul, Master Partridge. I expect them. I demand them."   85

His eyes grew hard as he spoke and blotches came into his grey cheeks. He saw his apprentice was defiant, and would keep his heart and soul for himself.

"It's five to eight, Mister Corbett, sir. I would be home—"

"What's your home to me, Master Partridge? What's your family and 90 friends to me when I've not got your heart and soul? For you're no use to me if I don't have all of you. There's a dribble of wet on that flask by your hand, Master Partridge. Wipe it off."

The wetness was a fresh-fallen tear, but the apprentice scorned to say so—even though others were beginning to leak out of his bitter eyes. 95

		Marks
(a)	What impressions do you get of Ben's friends from this extract?	2

(b) How do the first three paragraphs (lines 1-14) appropriately introduce and set the scene for what follows in the rest of the passage?   3

(c) What do you think the writer intended to suggest to you by each of the following?
    (i) He stared at the oak bench that shone with his sweat—and at the great stone mortar and pestle in which his spirit has been ground (lines 15-16)
    (ii) Huge wild shadows leaped among the retorts and crucibles (line 34)
    (iii) the description of the jars (lines 57-59)
    (iv) Slippered Mr Corbett was slunk down his stairs, quiet as a waistcoated rat (lines 63-64)   8

(d) Choose *two* words or phrases which you find particularly vivid. Comment on each of them so as to convey the reasons why you find them effective.   2

(e) What do you learn of Mr Corbett's character from each of the following?
    (i) Ben's reactions to his friends' fooling (lines 42-51)
    (ii) the author's description of Mr Corbett's physical appearance (lines 65-86)
    (iii) Mr Corbett's conversation with Ben (lines 62-93)   5

Total   20

Answer the questions opposite and then compare the quality of your work with the answers written below. These answers were written by a pupil under examination conditions.

Allow yourself an absolute maximum of 45 minutes for the five questions.

Before we look in detail at these answers we need to consider a few technical matters with regard to the marking.

You will see in the answers to this and to the other questions in this section that a tick is placed where a point is made. Each tick is worth one mark. In addition, plus signs are used to highlight material which might be given credit, but not necessarily a full mark. It may take one, two or even three plus signs before a full mark is given. Underlining and question marks indicate inaccuracy and/or irrelevance. No marks are lost where the odd slip of the pen causes an error of spelling or punctuation or grammar, but if such errors occurred very often they would be bound to lower the general quality of an answer.

Now to the answers themselves.

(a)   *His friends seem happy and carefree* ✓ *since they grin and wave on seeing Ben.*
      They also seem mischievous ✓ *as they enter the shop "with looks of cautious wickedness".*   2

Question (a) is easy. For 2 marks a completely different answer might point out the comic effect of Ben's friends and refer to the fact that they, unlike Ben, are free to come and go as they please.

(b)   *The first three paragraphs introduce the protagonists; both Ben and the apothecary are mentioned as are Ben's feelings towards him* (paragraph 3). *The reader also learns that Ben is in an apothecary's shop. The first paragraph, describing the past year, reflects the nature of the apothecary* ✓ *and the two are linked in paragraph 3. The reader is also introduced to Ben's desire to be home; it is New Year's Eve and the bad weather provides a contrast to celebrating at home.* ✓   3

The answer to (b) also gets full marks, though the question is more difficult. The answer might have included more detail by showing that the setting is funereal and eerie and therefore appropriate to the later mention of magic and witchcraft, that the bad weather creates an atmosphere of general misery and meanness, and that this in turn is reflected in the coldness and indifference of Mr Corbett's character. But the main issues are here and are written down with confidence.

(c)   (i)   *The writer suggests that Ben is oppressed* ✓ *by the apothecary; the sweat on the bench shows how hard he is made to work. He also suggests that the apothecary tries to enslave Ben by crushing his defiance and free will through work.* ✓
      (ii)   *The writer suggests that the shop is made strange and macabre as if the shadows were in some way supernatural.* ✓ *He also suggests that the dan-*

cing represents defiance since the apothecary wishes to crush the free *"wild"* spirit of Ben.

(iii)   The author suggests that Ben may be in trouble;/just as magistrates hand out punishments to wrongdoers so the apothecary may be angry with him. The jars are described as "fat" magistrates which provides <u>dramatic relief</u>[?] *to the diminutive Ben and his guilt is therefore suggested.*

(iv)   The author suggests that the appearance of Mr. Corbett is unexpected and sudden, "slunk", "quiet".✓ *It also suggests that he is sinister and unpleasant since "rat" suggests* <u>vermin</u>✓ *and the* <u>supernatural</u>[?]

6

(c) is also a good answer, scoring 6 out of a possible 8.

In (i) a good point, not fully brought out here, is that the instruments for crushing and grinding (the mortar and pestle) have crushed and ground down Ben himself.

In (ii) the point that the dancing represents defiance would certainly be worth a mark but for the fact that defiance has already been mentioned and rewarded in (i). Comment on the distortion of the shadows would be acceptable, as would any suggestion that the shadows are not merely shadows but evil beings with a life of their own.

In (iii) the pupil makes the central point about the jars judging Ben (in the idea of handing out punishments). Additional material might include: the fact that Ben is trapped and can't escape; magistrates are authoritative and overpowering; Ben appears small and insignificant and vulnerable.

Any reference to Mr Corbett's craftiness or cunning would be rewarded in (iv). An important omission from this answer is the failure to point out the bizarre and grotesque effect created by the linking of *waistcoated* and *rat*.

(d)   *"dying of an ague", is effective because it conveys the idea of a wind and tells us that the year is coming to an end. It brings to mind the* <u>traditional idea of Father Time</u> ?

   "Fitfully" is effective because it suggests that clouds pass over the moon, an idea which is linked to the supernatural. (How ?) It also suggests that the moon is affected by the same "ague" as the dying year.

0

(d) is disappointing, gaining no marks. The pupil misunderstands the meaning of *ague* and this invalidates his comment. His choice of *fitfully,* and the comment on it, are weak. But this answer does illustrate how very important it is, when given freedom of choice by a question, to make a good choice of word or phrase. Making a good choice means choosing something vivid, about which a proper comment can be made. It also means choosing something which is *not* covered by the requirements of other questions. It is as well, for example, to steer clear in answering (d) of choices and comments involving Mr Corbett, since his character is asked for in a later question, and there is no virtue (or reward) in saying the same thing twice.

Possible choices are:

line 17—*creak and groan like your shop sign.* This unusual comparison reveals Ben's desire for revenge and shows exactly what he thinks Mr Corbett deserves: pain and old age!

line 94—*fresh-fallen tear*. This observation evokes pity for Ben and suggests his youth and vulnerability.

Other possible choices include *pinkish flowers* (line 23) and *cautious wickedness* (lines 27-28). What can you say about each of these?

(e)   (i)   *We learn from this that Mr. Corbett is a tyrant;* ✓ *Ben is obviously afraid that he will hear and be angry. It also suggests that Mr. Corbett is attentive; he can be expected to hear from upstairs with a high wind blowing.*

       (ii)   *We learn that the apothecary is easily angered; his tight lips reveal his inner fury* ✓ *but he does not show his anger directly. His twitching cheek muscle suggests neurosis and therefore previous repression of anger. The apothecary's eye also reveals an unpleasant nature,* + *"swollen by spectacles".*

       (iii)   *The conversation tells us that Mr. Corbett is a mean killjoy;* ✓ *he will not even excuse Ben on New Year's Eve. He is also callous,* ✓ *"What's your home to me . . .?" He also wants to crush all defiance on Ben's part so that he becomes a mindless slave. This shows a sadistic and perverted character.* ✓ *He is obsessed with work* + *too. "What's half after seven when there's work to be done?"*

                                                           5

                                                        (16)

The answer to question (e) is one of those rare, full answers which actually has to be limited to the maximum number of marks available, though it deserves more.

(i) is straightforward and accurate.

(ii) mentions Mr Corbett's unpleasant nature, and could be put more strongly in terms of downright ugliness.

In (iii) the conversation reveals Mr Corbett as a Scrooge-like character, unreasonable, inhuman, and possessive. He is sinister and devilish: he wants Ben's soul! But the boy who has answered this question has done more than enough to gain full marks. Indeed, in a lesser answer, the plus signs on *unpleasant nature* and *obsessed with work* might each have gained a full mark.

Finally, notice the need for balance in answering questions. A question worth only 2 marks should be answered much more briefly than one which is worth 5 or 8.

Clearly, this is work of a high quality. To score 16 out of 20 puts this boy in the top flight of those attempting 'O' Level or 16+ examinations.

All of the answers are remarkable for their conciseness. They should prove to you that it is not necessary to write at great length in order to gain marks. Marks are given for what is accurate and relevant. This is the first lesson to learn.

2. Entering the City *by Tony Connor*

The city lies ahead. The vale
is cluttering as the train speeds through.
Hacked woods fall back; the scoop and swell
of cooling towers swing into view.

Acres of clinker, slag-heaps, roads   5
where lorries rev and tip all night,
railway sidings, broken sheds,
brutally bare in arc-light,

summon me to a present far
from Pericles's Athens, Caesar's Rome,   10
to follow again the river's scar
squirming beneath detergent foam.

I close the book, and rub the glass;
a glance ambiguously dark
entertains briefly scrap-yards, rows   15
of houses, and a treeless park,

like passing thoughts. Across my head
sundry familiar and strange
·denizens of the city tread
vistas I would, and would not, change.   20

Birth-place and home! The diesels' whine
flattens. Excited and defiled
once more, I heave the window down
and thrust my head out like a child.

denizen an inhabitant, a person who lives there
vista a view or prospect, especially along an avenue or across a
landscape

	Marks
(a) What are the poet's feelings about the city as revealed in the last two stanzas (lines 17-24)?	5

(b) Explain and comment on the following phrases:
    (i) ambiguously dark (line 14)
    (ii) a treeless park (line 16)   3

(c) What effects are created by each of the following?
    (i) the list of nouns in the second verse (lines 5-7)
    (ii) the reference to the cities of Athens and Rome (line 10)
    (iii) the diesels' whine/flattens (lines 21-22)   4

(d) Comment on the effectiveness of each of the following images:
- (i) The vale/is cluttering (lines 1-2)
- (ii) Hacked woods fall back (line 3)
- (iii) the river's scar/squirming beneath detergent foam (lines 11-12)   6

(e) What does the poem gain by being written in the present tense?   2

Total   20

Answer the above questions and then compare the quality of your work with the answers written below. These answers were written by a pupil under examination conditions.

Allow yourself an absolute maximum of 45 minutes for the five questions.

(a)   *The poet feels happiness and excitement yet at the same time dis-contentment as he enters the city in the train. His happy state of mind arises from the fact that he is returning to a familiar place ✓ which is home to him for he says "Birthplace and home" and calls the sights which meet his eyes "familiar". His eagerness and joy is apparent in the way that the poet exerts so much effort in pushing the window down just so that he can watch the city approaching and gain pleasure ✓ from such a childlike action. "I heave the window down" he says. In the second stanza the surroundings of the city are passing "across" the head of the poet, almost as if he is trying to take in too many sights all at once and instead of absorbing them, he only superficially appreciates them. His state of discontentment, however, is evident in the way in which the poet says that he would like to change some aspects of the city, ✓ and from this standpoint he does not just call the city his "home", but also his "birthplace", almost insinuating that he was brought up there and therefore is obliged to return.+ He furthermore talks about the deflating effect the whine of the diesel engines has upon him and calls himself "defiled" which <u>almost</u> ? suggests his disapproval.*   3

(a) gets 3 out of a possible 5 marks. The pupil has documented fully the poet's pleasurable feelings about the city, but has not recognised that these feelings are mixed with a wavering uncertainty, as shown by the phrases *would and would not, familiar and strange,* and, possibly, *Excited and defiled.* The city is his birthplace and home, but it is still disagreeable: it defiles him. It is a pity that the word *almost* is included in the last sentence of this answer; its omission would have brought an extra mark!

(b)   *(i) The phrase "ambiguously dark" suggests the drab surroundings which he views and also the indefinite forms ✓ which he sees. i.e. he merely sees a vague picture in a quick glance. There is also the suggestion that due to his absence from the city, he has forgotten the intricate details of the area.*
(ii) The phrase "treeless park" evokes an image well suited to the rest of his description. The word "treeless" suggests that the area is probably not a true park, but a patch of scrub ground ✓ with

89

*patches where no grass grows. It fits in well with the other nouns
he describes, as it suggests the barren and desert-like appearance
of an area which should be abundantly green.*✓ 3

(b) deservedly gets full marks.

(i) *ambiguously dark* is difficult, and this answer is as good as any. The mention of *drab
surroundings* is worth a mark, but since there are only 3 for the whole question, the mark
is given elsewhere in (ii). The word *ambiguously* shows that *dark* is dark in more than one
sense. Perhaps it refers not only to the city's grime and the indefinite forms seen at a
quick glance but also to the dark of the gathering twilight. (Or is it night? What clue
suggests this?)

(ii) *treeless park* is straightforward. An alternative comment about the destructive effect
of industry upon nature would be worth a mark.

(c)   *(i) The list of nouns in the second verse suggests the things that
he sees, while travelling past in the train. However, the effectiveness of the list technique is such that it conveys the continuity
of dullness ✓ and the cramped up conditions of a city area. The
nouns which he uses are all associated with man's industry + and
so help convey the continuous bustle of the city.
(ii) The reference to the cities of Athens and Rome acts as a
complete contrast to the conditions seen in this city. The cities of
Athens and Rome are associated with grandeur and wealth and
therefore very pointedly ✓ prove the contrast.
(iii) "The diesels' whine flattens" suggests that the train has
arrived at its destination i.e. the city and therefore is slowing down.
The word "whine" suggests almost a sense of tediousness felt by
the train + as it nears the railway station. The word "flattens" is
effective because it conveys the idea of the sound dying away.*✓   4

(c) is a fine answer, well worth the full 4 marks. Alternative material in (ii) might
compare the romance of these old, beautiful and legendary cities with the harsh reality
of a modern industrial city, or contrast culture with dullness.

In (iii) any comment suggesting that the diesels' whine is boring and monotonous would
be acceptable for a full mark in a less detailed answer.

(d)   *(i) This suggests the image of the banks of the vale almost
closing the train in, shutting out all other views.✓ The word "cluttering" indicates that the poet is not particularly impressed by
it + and would rather hurry on to his destination.
(ii) The image "Hacked woods fall back" is effective because it
conveys the idea of leaving behind woods as the train travels past
and also the idea that man and man's destructive influences are
moving out from the centre into the countryside.
(iii) Just as a wounded man might squirm from a freshly inflicted
wound so does the once freshwater river appear to writhe under
the burden of poisonous industrial effluent.✓ This image effectively*

shows how nature has once again suffered because of man ✓ *and progress in general; natural life, in this city at least, appears unable to exist because of the demand for further development.*   3

The answer to (d) is the weakest, scoring only half marks.

In (i) some reference to the haphazard industrial sprawl which has disfigured the vale would bring out more clearly the reason why the poet is not particularly impressed by it.

(ii) fails to comment on the image of *Hacked*. As the train speeds through the countryside the impression is given of it rapidly cutting down the trees. They *fall* back.

The answer to (iii) is good. The word *scar* is related to the idea of despoiling nature, and *squirming* suggests physical pain and an attempt to escape from torture.

(e)   *The present tense gives the poem a sort of immediacy, that this is what is going on right now.* ✓ *Furthermore it unites the concept of past, present and future, the past of the countryside he has left, the present of the city and the future in which he would like to see some alteration to the city, its appearance for example. The use of this tense suggests the joy and eagerness of the poet's arrival* ✓ *in the city, as his thoughts and feelings seem to run on and on.*   2

(15)

(e) is well done, apart from the pupil's comment about past, present and future, which is rather too fanciful and strained. Any reference to the idea of the reader actually being there with the poet, or to the fact that the past tense is less vivid, is worth a mark.

The poetry question generally causes the most difficulty in any English Literature examination. This answer, therefore, scoring 15 out of 20, is another very fine piece of work.

3. *From* **Mr Stone and the Knights Companion**
by V. S. Naipaul

It was Thursday, Miss Millington's afternoon off, and Mr Stone had
to let himself in. Before he could switch on the hall light, the depthless
green eyes held him, and in an instant the creature, eyes alone, leapt
down the steps. Mr Stone cowered against the dusty wall and shielded
his head with his briefcase. The cat brushed against his legs and was 5
out through the still open door. Mr Stone stood where he was, the
latchkey in one ungloved hand, and waited for the beating of his heart,
the radiation of fine pain through his body, to subside.

The cat belonged to the family next door, people who had moved into
the street just five years before and were still viewed by Mr Stone with 10
suspicion. It had come to the house as a kitten, a pet for the children;
and as soon as, ceasing to chase paper and ping-pong balls and balls of
string, it began to dig up Mr Stone's garden, its owners having no
garden worth digging up, Mr Stone had transferred his hostility from
the family to their cat. When he returned from the office he examined 15
his flowerbeds—strips of earth between irregular areas of crazy
paving—for signs of the animal's obscene scuttlings and dredgings
and buryings. "Miss Millington! Miss Millington!" he would call.
"The cat pepper!" And heavy old Miss Millington, aproned down to
her ankles, would shuffle out with a large tin of pepper dust (originally 20
small tins had been thought sufficient: the picture of the terrified cat
on the label looked so convincing) and would ritually sprinkle all the
flowerbeds, the affected one more than the others, as though to
obscure rather than prevent the animal's activities. In time the
flowerbeds had become discoloured; it was as if cement had been 25
mixed with the earth and dusted on to the leaves and stems of plants.

Now the cat had penetrated into the house itself.

The beating of Mr Stone's heart moderated and the shooting pain
receded, leaving a trail of exposed nerves, a lightness of body below
the heavy Simpson's overcoat, and an urge to decisive action. Not 30
closing the front door, turning on no lights, not taking off his overcoat
or hat, depositing only his gloves and briefcase on the hall table, he
went to the kitchen, where in darkness he opened the larder door and
took out the cheese, still in its Sainsbury wrapping, from its accus-
tomed place—Miss Millington shopped on Thursday mornings. He 35
found a knife and carefully, as though preparing cocktail savouries,
chopped the cheese into small cubes. These he took outside, to the
front gate; and glancing about him in the sodden murk—some windows alight, no observer about—he laid a trail of cheese from gate to
door, up the dark carpeted hall, now bitterly cold, and up the steps to 40
the bathroom. Here, sitting on the cover of the lavatory bowl, still in
his hat and overcoat, he waited, poker in hand. The poker was not for
attack but self-defence. Often, walking down that cat-infested street,
he had been surprised by a cat sitting sedately on a fence post at the

level of his head, and he had always made as if to shield his face. It was 45
a disgraceful action, but one he could never control. He feared the
creatures; and there were all those stories of cornered cats, of cats
growing wild and attacking men.

The damp air filled the hall and invaded the bathroom. The darkness
and the silence emphasized the cold. He had visions of dipping the 50
cat's paws in boiling oil, of swinging the creature by its tail and
flinging it down to the pavement below, of scalding it in boiling water.
He got up from the lavatory seat and turned on the geyser. Instant hot
water! The water ran cold, then after the *whoomph!* as the jets caught,
lukewarm, then at last warm. The geyser needed cleaning; he must 55
remind Miss Millington. He filled the basin and sat down again on the
lavatory bowl. The water-pipes ceased to hum; silence returned.

Some minutes later, five, perhaps ten, he remembered. It was rats that
ate cheese. Cats ate other things. He put on lights everywhere, closed
the front door, and turned on fires.   60

The cheese he forgot. It was a pleasurably agitated Miss Millington
who reported the next morning on the disappearance of her cheese
from the larder, and its conversion into cubes laid in a wavering line
from gate to bathroom. He offered no explanation.

		Marks

(a)   What impressions do you get of Mr Stone from this passage? Refer to
details in the passage in support of your answer.   5

(b)   Why does the writer give the sentence in line 27 a paragraph to itself?   2

(c)   Explain and comment on each of the following phrases:
    (i)   the radiation of fine pain (line 8)
    (ii) that cat-infested street (line 43)
    (iii) pleasurably agitated (line 61)   6

(d)   Comment on lines 15-26, including the words in brackets, in order to
bring out how the writer gently pokes fun at Miss Millington and Mr
Stone.   4

(e)   How successful do you find the last paragraph (lines 61-64) as a conclusion to this episode? Give reasons.   3

                                                             Total   20

Answer the above questions and then compare the quality of your work with the
answers written below. These answers were written by a pupil under examination
conditions.

Allow yourself an absolute maximum of 45 minutes for the five questions.

(a)   *The first description of Mr. Stone's actions, the fact that he "cowered"
against the wall and "shielded" his head with his briefcase straight-away
sets him as being an odd character because of his unusual behaviour. The
fact that this brief encounter with a cat makes his heart beat sending a
"radiation of fine pain through his body" seems rather an over-dramatic
way to act and makes him appear weak and cowardly.✓ This is backed up
by his having to call for Miss Millington to bring the "cat pepper". His
beating heart subsiding to leave a "trail of exposed nerves" and a "lightness
of body" shows how ridiculous✓ he is to be so easily disturbed. The
cat obviously annoys him greatly to such an extent that he is made to
leave a trail of cheese for it and wait in the bathroom with a poker for "self
defence". It is here that the fact he is eccentric✓ is confirmed. His ideas for
punishing the cat only emphasise how absurdly ridiculous he is. (repetition)
The description of the geyser and his having to remind Miss Millington
that it needs cleaning shows how incoherent and how rambling his mind is.+*   3

The answer to (a) is fair, but there are notable omissions and some repetition. The girl
who wrote this answer says that Mr Stone is *an odd character*, but this is not really precise
enough and it is not until we reach *eccentric* that the mark is given. He is somewhat
insular and doesn't get on well with people, as is shown by his hostility to the
neighbours. He is certainly absent-minded, as shown by his confusion of cats and rats
and forgetting the cheese, and it could be argued that the fuss he makes over a small
amount of garden and his cutting of the cheese into small cubes show a pathetic
preoccupation with trifling details. An obvious but valid point is that he is obsessed with
cats. His phobia about them makes him wildly imaginative and vengeful.

(b)   *The writer gives the sentence a paragraph to itself in order to make more
dramatic✓ the statement. After the long winded descriptions of the previous
paragraph? the simplicity and shortness of the statement emphasises the
meaning and prepares the reader for what is to come.✓*   2

(b) is a concise answer, though it is inaccurate to say that the descriptions of the previous
paragraph are *long-winded*. Rather they are important in recounting the history of
events leading up to line 27.

Alternative material might include any statement that the sentence adds emphasis to the
action the cat is now taking: it becomes a sinister development. It also exposes Mr
Stone's horrified reaction.

(c)   *(i)   "the radiation of fine pain" is referring to the beating of his heart
quickening as the cat has touched him. It doesn't hurt him because it is
described as "fine" but this word effectively conveys the irritation he feels
towards the cat's presence.✓/The word "radiation" suggests the annoyance
spreading/through his body.
(ii)   The phrase "that cat infested street" again conveys Mr. Stone's
feeling of hatred towards cats which has come about through the single cat
disrupting his garden and now his house. The use of the word "infested",
seems to be an exaggeration✓ as the word is usually applied to phrases
such as "shark infested seas". To Mr. Stone, therefore, the cats have taken
on an image similar to something as horrific and frightening✓ as sharks
for example. (or vermin?)
(iii)   The phrase "pleasurably agitated", gives us some indication as to*

> *Miss Millington's character; the words in fact seem to contradict each other,✓ but because there is a trail of cheese it gives Miss Millington something to create a fuss about which she obviously enjoys.✓*   6

(c) is splendid work, earning full marks. There is little to add here, except perhaps that in (ii) some reference to vermin or pests would probably be more appropriate than *sharks*. Mr Stone's hatred of cats (not rewarded here) is a simple point.

In (iii) Miss Millington is *pleasurably agitated* because the mystery of the cheese is a departure from routine. She is determined to fuss about it.

(d)   *The fact that the "flowerbeds" are described as being "strips of earth between irregular areas of crazy paving" makes the description of the fuss the two people make about it, which is described later, seem faintly ridiculous.✓ The use of the word "obscene" to describe the cat's "scuttl- ings" and "dredgings" is an over-exaggerated way of describing a cat playing in some soil and therefore suggests the mocking attitude✓ of the author. Miss Millington's movements being that of a "shuffle" and the description of the "terrified" cat on the tin of pepper, plus the fact that she "ritually" sprinkles the flowerbeds show the writer poking fun because the seriousness with which all this is described makes them appear all the more absurd.✓*   3

In (d) there is a lot of material available for the 4 marks. This pupil obtains 3 marks, but for her last mark groups together three ideas (Miss Millington's shuffling, the terrified cat, the ritual sprinkling) in order to make only one collective comment about them. Each of these ideas could be commented on separately, and this would have brought extra marks. Their acceptance of the picture of the terrified cat, for example, and their purchase of larger tins when smaller tins of the same cat pepper have proved ineffectual, show how gullible Mr Stone and Miss Millington are.

Notice that Mr Stone succeeds only in destroying his own garden, which is foolish when he is so particular about it. Miss Millington's actions reveal an inept and simple old lady who treats flowerbeds which have already been attacked rather more thoroughly than those which haven't—a futile occupation.

(e)   *The last paragraph is very effective because it emphasises the absurdity of the pair. The fact that Miss Millington is described as having "reported" the "conversion" of the cheese into a "wavering" line, all these words suggest the humour+ of the passage and so add to its effectiveness. The fact that it starts with such a short sentence draws your attention to the last few lines + and the also short and abrupt last sentence successfully rounds off the passage because there is nothing more to be said.✓*   2

(16)

(e) obtains 2 of the 3 marks available. The point about the humour may be true, but it doesn't really affect the paragraph *as a conclusion*, which is what was asked for. Further comment, too, about Mr Stone's character is likely to be irrelevant. Those who don't find the paragraph successful as a conclusion might point out that it is something of an anti-climax: Mr Stone fails to trap the cat and therefore the episode is not concluded at all; but this would be a weak comment. Do we seriously expect his "plan" to succeed?

The main point, for the third mark, is that Miss Millington is denied the knowledge that the reader has gained about Mr Stone and the cheese, and it is always satisfying to a reader to obtain this advantage over one of the characters in a novel.

One final general point. In English Literature, as you have seen, you are often asked questions about *the effectiveness* of words and phrases.

When answering such questions, be guided by these three simple rules:

1) **Never** write:

This word (or this phrase) *is very good* or *This word* (or this phrase) *is very effective* and leave it at that. It says nothing.

If you must start in this way, follow it with a reason. For example: *This word is very effective because* . . .

2) **Always** try to use your imagination and write about what the words *suggest* to you.

Don't just give their meaning. That's the job of a dictionary.

3) **Beware** of paraphrase, that is, writing out what the author has already written without making any imaginative comment of your own.

In the last section of this book, SECTION D, there are twenty test papers based on ten prose passages and ten poems. They have all been chosen because of their high quality and because of their interest, variety and appeal.

Some of the questions are quite hard to answer well, but they are typical of the sort of question which is set in 'O' Level, 16+ and CSE examinations, and it is hoped that your teacher will offer guidance where appropriate. All of the passages and poems are suitable for class discussion as well as, or prior to, written work.

If you accept the challenge of trying to produce answers of high quality—as the pupils who have contributed to this section have done—you will find that the questions will enable you to understand in more depth, and to enjoy more fully, the skills of fine writing.

1. *From* **Sons and Lovers** *by D. H. Lawrence*

The kitchen was full of the scent of boiled herbs and hops. On the hob
a large black saucepan steamed slowly. Mrs. Morel took a panchion, a
great bowl of thick red earth, streamed a heap of white sugar into the
bottom, and then, straining herself to the weight, was pouring in the
liquor.   5

Just then Morel came in. He had been very jolly in the Nelson, but
coming home had grown irritable; and a bad conscience afflicted him
as he neared the house. He did not know he was angry. But when the
garden-gate resisted his attempts to open it, he kicked it and broke the
latch. He entered just as Mrs. Morel was pouring the infusion of herbs 10
out of the saucepan. Swaying slightly, he lurched against the table.
The boiling liquor pitched. Mrs. Morel started back.

"Good gracious," she cried, "coming home in his drunkenness!"

"Comin' home in his what?" he snarled, his hat over his eye.

Suddenly her blood rose in a jet.   15

"Say you're *not* drunk!" she flashed.

She had put down her saucepan, and was stirring the sugar into the
beer. He dropped his two hands heavily on the table, and thrust his
face forward at her.

"Say you're not drunk," he repeated. "Why nobody but a nasty little 20
bitch like you 'ud 'ave such a thought."

He thrust his face forward at her.

"There's money to bezzle with, if there's money for nothing else."

"I've not spent a two-shillin' bit this day," he said.

"You don't get as drunk as a lord on nothing," she replied. "And," 25
she cried, flashing into sudden fury, "if you've been sponging on your
beloved Jerry, why, let him look after his children, for they need it."

"It's a lie, it's a lie. Shut your face, woman."

They were now at battle-pitch. Each forgot everything save the hatred of the other and the battle between them. She was fiery and furious as 30 he. They went on till he called her a liar.

"No," she cried, starting up, scarce able to breathe. "Don't call me that—you, the most despicable liar that ever walked in shoe-leather." She forced the last words out of suffocated lungs.

"You're a liar!" he yelled, banging the table with his fist. "You're a 35 liar, you're a liar."

She stiffened herself with clenched fists.

"The house is filthy with you," she cried.

"Then get out on it—it's mine. Get out on it!" he shouted. "It's me as brings th' money whoam, not thee. It's my house, not thine. Then get 40 out on't—get out on't!"

"And I would," she cried, suddenly shaken into tears of impotence. "Ah, wouldn't I, wouldn't I have gone long ago, but for those children. Ay, haven't I repented not going years ago, when I'd only the one"—suddenly drying into rage. "Do you think it's for *you* I stop— 45 do you think I'd stop one minute for *you*?"

"Go then," he shouted, beside himself. "Go!"

"No!" she faced round. "No," she cried loudly, "you shan't have it *all* your own way; you shan't do *all* you like. I've got those children to see to. My word," she laughed, "I should look well to leave them to 50 you."

"Go," he cried thickly, lifting his fist. He was afraid of her. "Go!"

"I should be only too glad. I should laugh, laugh, my lord, if I could get away from you," she replied.

He came up to her, his red face, with its bloodshot eyes, thrust 55 forward and gripped her arms. She cried in fear of him, struggled to be free. Coming slightly to himself, panting, he pushed her roughly to the outer door, and thrust her forth, slotting the bolt behind her with a bang. Then he went back into the kitchen, dropped into his armchair, his head, bursting full of blood, sinking between his knees. Thus he 60 dipped gradually into a stupor, from exhaustion and intoxication.

(a)　What different aspects of Morel's character are revealed by any FOUR of the following?

    (i)　*a bad conscience afflicted him* (line 7)

    (ii)　*he kicked it and broke the latch* (lines 9-10)

    (iii)　*a nasty little bitch like you* (lines 20-21)

    (iv)　*You're a liar! he yelled, banging the table with his fist. You're a liar, you're a liar.* (lines 35-36)

    (v)　*It's me as brings th' money whoam, not thee* (lines 39-40)

    (vi)　*lifting his fist* (line 52)　　　　　　　　　　　　　　　6

(b)　What evidence can you find in the text to support the view that Mrs Morel must take some of the blame for the outbreak of the argument?　　2

(c)　Can you suggest any reason why Morel was *afraid of her* (line 52)?　　2

(d)　What effects are created by each of the following?

    (i)　the first paragraph (lines 1-5)

    (ii)　the use of words such as *cried—flashed—snarled—fury—yelled—shouted—rage.*

    (iii)　*shaken into tears of impotence* (line 42)

    (iv)　the emphasis upon dialogue rather than narration (apart from the opening and concluding paragraphs)

    (v)　the mood of the last two sentences　　　　　　　　　10

　　　　　　　　　　　　　　　　　　　　　　　Total　20

2.　**At 30,000 Feet** *by Bernard Gilhooly*

A fleck of silver against the darkening blue
The hollow cylinder rockets under the sky's dome,
Unavailingly pursued by the thunder of its sound
Until that final scarlet reverberation;
Like the telegraphed words burning meaninglessly　　　　5
Upon the slip of yellow paper, and the explosion
Of grief within the mind, this fire and thunder
Do not quite coincide:
The eyes of the watcher see the disaster
Before its voice awakens in his ear.　　　　　　　10

Nothing that has meaning descends again to earth;
The lighted runway waits vainly
To feel the screeching tyres;
Customs officials will not search this baggage
That downward flakes in dust on silent fields;　　　　15
Hands cannot clasp, nor lips press
What is now blown weightlessly about the sky.

There was a moment when they drowsed
Deep in luxurious chairs;
Read magazines, wrote letters;   20
When stewardesses served coffee and liqueurs,
And dirty dishes were neatly stacked
In the bright kitchen.

No other moment followed;
Time stopped. There was nothing . . .   25

No doubt there is a meaning to this event;
But not the one that can be read
On the white face of the farmer
In mid-furrow gazing upward from his plough,
Nor in the burned minds of those who wait   30
At the airport barrier.

Marks

(a)   What does the poet mean by *this fire and thunder* (line 7)? To what is *this fire and thunder* being compared?   4

(b)   How is a sense of comfort and of purposeful routine created in the third stanza (lines 18-23)?   4

(c)   Bring out the effectiveness of each of the following phrases:
    (i)   *the explosion/Of grief within the mind* (lines 6-7)
    (ii) *downward flakes in dust on silent fields* (line 15)
    (iii) *burned minds* (line 30)   6

(d)   Comment on the effectiveness of the poet's use of any TWO adjectives in the poem.   2

(e)   What is the poet's attitude to the disaster, as shown in the last stanza (lines 26-31)?   2

(f)   How successful is the poem in its evocation of an aircraft disaster?   2

Total   20

3.   *From* **Holiday Memory** *by Dylan Thomas*

Dusk came down; or grew up out of the sands and the sea; or curled around us from the calling docks and the bloodily smoking sun. The day was done, the sands brushed and ruffled suddenly with a sea-broom of cold wind.

And we gathered together all the spades and buckets and towels, 5
empty hampers and bottles, umbrellas and fish-frails, bats and balls and knitting, and went—oh, listen, Dad!—to the fair in the dusk on the bald seaside field.

Fairs were no good in the day; then they were shoddy and tired; the voices of hoop-la girls were crimped as elocutionists; no cannon-ball 10 could shake the roosting coconuts; the gondolas mechanically repeated their sober lurch; the Wall of Death was safe as a governess cart; the wooden animals were waiting for the night.

But in the night, the hoop-la girls, like operatic crows, croaked at the coming moon; whizz, whirl, and ten for a tanner, the coconuts rained 15 from their sawdust like grouse from the Highland sky; tipsy the griffin-prowed gondolas weaved on dizzy rails and the Wall of Death was a spinning rim of ruin, and the neighing wooden horses took, to a haunting hunting tune, a thousand Becher's Brooks as easily and breezily as hooved swallows. 20

Approaching, at dusk, the fair-field from the beach, we scorched and gritty boys heard above the belabouring of the batherless sea the siren voices of the raucous, horsy barkers.

"Roll up, roll up!"

In her tent and her rolls of flesh the Fattest Woman in the World sat 25 sewing her winter frock, another tent, and fixed her little eyes, blackcurrants in blancmange, on the skeletons who filed and sniggered by.

"Roll up, roll up, roll up to see the Largest Rat on Earth, the Rover or Bonzo of vermin." 30

Here scampered the smallest pony, like a Shetland shrew. And here "The Most Intelligent Fleas," trained, reined, bridled, and bitted, minutely cavorted in their glass corral.

Round galleries and shies and stalls, pennies were burning holes in a hundred pockets. 35

Pale young men with larded hair and Valentino-black side-whiskers, fags stuck to their lower lips, squinted along their swivel-sighted rifles and aimed at ping-pong balls dancing on fountains.

Outside his booth stood a bitten-eared and barndoor-chested pug with a nose like a twisted swede and hair that started from his eyebrows and 40 three teeth yellow as a camel's inviting any sportsman to a sudden and sickening basting in the sandy ring or a quid if he lasted a round; and, wiry, cocky, bow-legged, coal-scarred, boozed sportsmen by the dozen strutted in and reeled out; and still those three teeth remained, chipped and camel-yellow in the bored, teak face. 45

Draggled and stout-wanting mothers, with haphazard hats, hostile hatpins, buns awry, bursting bags, and children at their skirts like pop-filled and jam-smeared limpets, screamed before distorting mirrors, at their suddenly tapering or tubular bodies and huge ballooning heads, and the children gaily bellowed at their own reflected bodies 50 withering and bulging in the glass.

Girls in skulled and cross-boned tunnels shrieked, and were comforted.

Young men, heroic after pints, stood up on the flying chairoplanes, tousled, crimson, and against the rules.   55

Jaunty girls gave sailors sauce.

All the fun of the fair in the hot, bubbling night. The man in the sand-yellow moon over the hurdy of gurdies. The swing-boats swimming to and fro like slices of the moon. Dragons and hippogriffs at the prows of the gondolas breathing fire and Sousa. Midnight roundabout 60 riders tantivying under the fairy-lights, huntsmen on billygoats and zebras hallooing under a circle of glow-worms.

And as we climbed home, up the gas-lit hill, to the still homes over the mumbling bay, we heard the music die and the voices drift like sand. And we saw the lights of the fair fade. And, at the far end of the seaside 65 field, they lit their lamps, one by one, in the caravans.

		Marks
(a)	How does the writer convey the differences between the fair in the daytime and the fair by night (lines 9-20)?	3

(b)	Comment on the effectiveness of each of the following:
	  (i) the image of dusk (lines 1-2)
	  (ii) *oh, listen, Dad!* (line 7)
	  (iii) *scorched and gritty boys* (lines 21-22)
	  (iv) any ONE simile of your own choice
		8

(c)	How does the writer make fun of the Fattest Woman in the World (lines 25-28)?	2
(d)	By commenting on THREE details of the description of the boxer (lines 39-45), show how his strength and toughness are conveyed.	3
(e)	What contrasts in mood and atmosphere do you detect between the last two paragraphs (lines 57-62 and 63-66)?	2
(f)	What is distinctive about the style in which the passage is written?	2
	Total	20

4. **A Glasgow Sonnet** by *Edwin Morgan*

A mean wind wanders through the backcourt trash.
Hackles on puddles rise, old mattresses
puff briefly and subside. Play-fortresses
of brick and bric-à-brac spill out some ash.
Four storeys have no windows left to smash,   5
but in the fifth a chipped sill buttresses
mother and daughter the last mistresses
of that black block condemned to stand, not crash.
Around them the cracks deepen, the rats crawl.
The kettle whimpers on a crazy hob.   10
Roses of mould grow from ceiling to wall.
The man lies late since he has lost his job,
smokes on one elbow, letting his coughs fall
thinly into an air too poor to rob.

Marks

(a) How do the first nine lines of the poem establish an unpleasant and
depressing atmosphere?   6

(b) What is meant by *condemned to stand* (line 8)?   2

(c) Explain and bring out the effectiveness of each of the following images:
    (i)   *Hackles on puddles rise* (line 2)
    (ii) *buttresses* (line 6)
    (iii) *whimpers* (line 10)
    (iv) *Roses of mould* (line 11)   8

(d) Show how the poet conveys a sense of futility and despair in the last three
lines of the poem.   4

Total   20

5. *From* **Washington Square** *by Henry James (adapted)*

Catherine listened for her father when he came in that evening, and
she heard him go to his study. She sat quiet, though her heart was
beating fast, for nearly half an hour; then she went and knocked at his
door—a ceremony without which she never crossed the threshold of
this apartment. On entering it now, she found him in his chair beside 5
the fire, entertaining himself with a cigar and the evening paper.

"I have something to say to you," she began very gently; and she sat
down in the first place that offered.

"I shall be very happy to hear it, my dear," said her father. He
waited—waited, looking at her—while she stared, in a long silence, at 10
the fire. He was curious and impatient, for he was sure she was going
to speak of Morris Townsend; but he let her take her own time, for he
was determined to be very mild.

"I am engaged to be married!" Catherine announced at last, still
staring at the fire.   15

The Doctor was startled; the accomplished fact was more than he had
expected; but he betrayed no surprise. "You do right to tell me," he
simply said. "And who is the happy mortal whom you have honoured
with your choice?"

"Mr Morris Townsend." And as she pronounced her lover's name 20
Catherine looked at him. What she saw was her father's still grey eye
and his clear-cut, definite smile. She contemplated these objects for a
moment, and then she looked back at the fire; it was much warmer.

"Is it serious?" said the Doctor.

"Very serious, father."   25

Her father glanced at her an instant, removing his eyes from the fire.
"I don't wonder Mr Townsend likes you; you are so simple and
good."

"I feel very old—and very wise," said Catherine, smiling faintly.

"I am afraid that before long you will feel older and wiser yet. I don't 30
like your engagement."

"Ah!" Catherine exclaimed, softly, getting up from her chair.

"No, my dear. I am sorry to give you pain; but I don't like it. You
should have consulted me before you settled it. I have been too easy
with you, and I feel as if you had taken advantage of my indulgence. 35
Most decidedly you should have spoken to me first."

Catherine hesitated a moment, and then—"It was because I was afraid
you wouldn't like it," she confessed.

"You were quite right. I don't like him."

"Dear father, you don't know him," said Catherine, in a voice so 40
timidly argumentative that it might have touched him.

"Very true. I don't know him intimately. But I know him enough; I
have my impression of him."

"I know what you mean," said Catherine, remembering how Morris
had forewarned her. "You mean that he is mercenary."   45

The Doctor smiled a little. "Very true. There is, of course, nothing
impossible in a young man entertaining a disinterested affection for
you. You are an honest, amiable girl, and an intelligent young man

might easily find it out. But the principal thing that we know about this young man—who is, indeed, very intelligent—leads us to suppose 50 that, however much he may value your personal merits, he values your money more. The principal thing we know about him is that he has led a life of dissipation, and has spent a fortune of his own in doing so. That is enough for me, my dear. I wish you to marry a young man with other antecedents—a young man who could give positive guarantees. 55 If Morris Townsend has spent his own fortune in amusing himself, there is every reason to believe that he would spend yours."

The Doctor delivered himself of these remarks slowly, deliberately, with occasional pauses and prolongations of accent, which made no great allowance for poor Catherine's suspense as to his conclusion. She 60 sat down at last, with her head bent and her eyes still fixed upon him. There was something hopeless and oppressive in having to argue with her father. He was so quiet; he was not at all angry; and she, too, must be quiet. But her very effort to be quiet made her tremble.

"That is not the principal thing we know about him," she said; and 65 there was a touch of her tremor in her voice. "There are other things—many other things. He has very high abilities—he wants so much to do something. He is kind, and generous, and true," said poor Catherine, who had not suspected hitherto the resources of her eloquence. "And his fortune—his fortune that he spent—was very 70 small."

"All the more reason he shouldn't have spent it," cried the Doctor, getting up with a laugh. Then, as Catherine, who has also risen to her feet again, stood there in her rather angular earnestness, wishing so much and expressing so little, he drew her towards him and kissed 75 her. "You won't think me cruel?" he said, holding her a moment.

		Marks
(a)	How does the writer convey Catherine's unease in the first two paragraphs (lines 1-8)?	2
(b)	What impressions of the Doctor do you derive from this passage?	6

(c)	Explain carefully the meaning of each of the following expressions:
	   (i) *it was much warmer* (line 23)
	   (ii) *timidly argumentative* (line 41)
	   (iii) *her rather angular earnestness* (line 74)
		6

(d)	What evidence is there in the passage to support the Doctor's claims about Morris Townsend?	2
(e)	In what ways does Catherine respond to her father's criticisms of her fiancé?	4
	Total	20

6. The Wasps' Nest *by James L. Rosenberg*

Two aerial tigers,
Striped in ebony and gold
And resonantly, savagely a-hum,
Have lately come
To my mail-box's metal hold   5
And thought
With paper and with mud
Therein to build
Their insubstantial and their only home.
Neither the sore displeasure   10
Of the U.S. Mail
Nor all my threats and warnings
Will avail
To turn them from their hummed devotions.
And I think   15
They know my strength,
Can gauge
The danger of their work:
One blow could crush them
And their nest; and I am not their friend.   20
And yet they seem
Too deeply and too fiercely occupied
To bother to attend.
Perhaps they sense
I'll never deal the blow,   25
For, though not in nor of them,
Still I think I know
What it is like to live
In an alien and gigantic universe, a stranger,
Building fragile citadels of love   30
On the edge of danger.

Marks

(a) The poem consists of five sentences. Summarise briefly each of these five sentences in order to bring out clearly the poem's meaning.   6

(b) Explain and comment on the effectiveness of each of the following:
    (i) *two aerial tigers* (line 1)
    (ii) *Their insubstantial and their only home* (line 9)
    (iii) *the sore displeasure/Of the U.S. Mail* (lines 10-11)
    (iv) *hummed devotions* (line 14)   8

(c) Comment on the variety of line length used in the poem.   1

(d) What comparisons are made in the last three lines of the poem? What do these comparisons reveal of the poet's attitude to the wasps?   5

Total   20

7. *From* **Memoirs of an Infantry Officer** *by Siegfried Sassoon*

Every afternoon at half-past five the School assembled to listen to a lecture. Eyeing an audience of about 300 officers and N.C.O.s, I improved my knowledge of regimental badges, which seemed somehow to affect the personality of the wearer. A lion, a lamb, a dragon or an antelope, a crown, a harp, a tiger or a sphinx, these devices 5 differentiated men in more ways than one. There was food for thought also in the fact of sitting between a Connaught Ranger and a Seaforth Highlander, though both were likely to have been born in Middlesex. Queer, too, was the whole scene in that schoolroom, containing as it did a splendid sample of the Fourth Army which began the Somme 10 Battle a couple of months afterwards.

My woolgatherings were cut short when the lecturer cleared his throat; the human significance of the audience was obliterated then, and its outlook on life became restricted to destruction and defence. A gas expert from G.H.Q. would inform us that "gas was still in its 15 infancy". (Most of us were either dead or disabled before gas had had time to grow up.) An urbane Artillery General assured us that high explosive would be our best friend in future battles, and his ingratiating voice made us unmindful, for the moment, that explosives often arrived from the wrong direction. But the star turn in the schoolroom 20 was a massive sandy-haired Highland Major whose subject was "The Spirit of the Bayonet". Though at that time undecorated, he was afterwards awarded the D.S.O. for lecturing. He took as his text a few leading points from the *Manual of Bayonet Training*.

> "To attack with the bayonet effectively requires Good Direction, 25 Strength and Quickness, during a state of wild excitement and probably physical exhaustion. The bayonet is essentially an offensive weapon. In a bayonet assault all ranks go forward to kill or be killed, and only those who have developed skill and strength by constant training will be able to kill. The spirit of the bayonet must 30 be inculcated into all ranks, so that they go forward with that aggressive determination and confidence of superiority born of continual practice, without which a bayonet assault will not be effective."

He spoke with homicidal eloquence, keeping the game alive with 35 genial and well-judged jokes. He had a Sergeant to assist him. The Sergeant, a tall sinewy machine, had been trained to such a pitch of frightfulness that at a moment's warning he could divest himself of all semblance of humanity. With rifle and bayonet he illustrated the Major's ferocious aphorisms, including facial expression. When told 40 to "put on the killing face", he did so, combining it with an ultra-vindictive attitude. "To instil fear into the opponent" was one of the Major's main maxims. Man, it seemed, had been created to jab the life out of Germans. To hear the Major talk, one might have thought that he did it himself every day before breakfast. 45

Afterwards I went up the hill to my favourite sanctuary, a wood of hazels and beeches. The evening air smelt of wet mould and wet leaves; the trees were misty-green; the church bell was tolling in the town, and smoke rose from the roofs. Peace was there in the twilight of that prophetic foreign spring. But the lecturer's voice still battered on 50 my brain. "The bullet and the bayonet are brother and sister." "If you don't kill him, he'll kill you." "Stick him between the eyes, in the throat, in the chest." "Don't waste good steel. Six inches are enough. What's the use of a foot of steel sticking out at the back of a man's neck? Three inches will do for him; when he coughs, go and look for 55 another."

Marks

(a) Comment on (i) the description of the Highland Major (lines 20-45) and (ii) the description of the Sergeant who assists him (lines 36-42) in order to bring out the writer's contempt for those who wage war.   6

(b) What does the extract from the *Manual of Bayonet Training* add to the atmosphere of the passage?   3

(c) By referring to TWO examples, comment on the writer's sense of humour.   2

(d) What contrasting effects are created by the last paragraph (lines 46-56)?   4

(e) What impressions of the character of the writer do you derive from this passage?   5

Total   20

8. **Little City** *by Robert Horan*

Spider, from his flaming sleep,
staggers out into the window frame;
swings out from the red den where he slept
to nest in the gnarled glass.
Fat hero, burnished cannibal   5
lets down a frail ladder and ties a knot,
sways down to a landing with furry grace.

By noon this corner is a bullet-coloured city
and the exhausted architect
sleeps in his pale wheel,   10
waits without pity for a gold visitor
or coppery captive, his aerial enemies
spinning headlong down the window to the trap.

The street of string shakes now and announces
a surprised angel in the tunnel of thread.   15
Spider dances down his wiry heaven to taste the moth.

A little battle begins and the prison trembles.
The round spider hunches like a judge.
The wheel glistens.
But this transparent town that caves in at a breath   20
is paved with perfect steel.
The victim hangs by his feet, and the spider
circles invisible avenues, weaving a grave.

By evening the web is heavy with monsters,
bright constellation of wasps and bees,   25
breathless, surrendered.
Bronze skeletons dangle on the wires
and a thin wing flutters.
The medieval city hangs in its stars.

Spider lumbers down the web   30
and the city stretches with the weight of his walking.
By night we cannot see the flies' faces
and the spider, rocking.

Marks

(a)   In what ways does the poet suggest the sinister and menacing nature
       of the spider?   4

(b)   What other aspects of the spider are suggested by each of the following?
       (i)   *Fat hero* (line 5)
       (ii)   *with furry grace* (line 7)
       (iii) *exhausted architect* (line 9)   6

(c)   Bring out the effectiveness of the sustained comparison of the web to a
       city (lines 8, 14, 20-23).   4

(d)   Explain and bring out the effectiveness of TWO of the following images:
       (i)   the comparison of the moth to *a surprised angel* (line 15)
       (ii)   *his wiry heaven* (line 16)
       (iii) *heavy with monsters* (line 24)   4

(e)   Explain carefully what is meant by the phrase *bright constellation of wasps
       and bees* (line 25). How is this phrase related to *The medieval city hangs in
       its stars* (line 29)?   2

Total   20

9.   *From* **Down and Out in Paris and London** *by George Orwell*

Our cafeterie was a murky cellar measuring twenty feet by seven by
eight high, and so crowded with coffee-urns, breadcutters and the like
that one could hardly move without banging against something. It was
lighted by one dim electric bulb, and four or five gas-fires that sent out
a fierce red breath. There was a thermometer there, and the temp- 5

erature never fell below 110 degrees Fahrenheit—it neared 130 at some times of the day. At one end were five service lifts, and at the other an ice cupboard where we stored milk and butter. When you went into the ice cupboard you dropped a hundred degrees of temp- erature at a single step; it used to remind me of the hymn about 10 Greenland's icy mountains and India's coral strand. Two men worked in the cafeterie besides Boris and myself. One was Mario, a huge, excitable Italian—he was like a city policeman with operatic gestures—and the other, a hairy, uncouth animal whom we called the Magyar; I think he was a Transylvanian, or something even more 15 remote. Except the Magyar we were all big men, and at the rush hour we collided incessantly.

The work in the cafeterie was spasmodic. We were never idle, but the real work only came in bursts of two hours at a time—we called each burst *"un coup de feu."* The first *coup de feu* came at eight, when the 20 guests upstairs began to wake up and demand breakfast. At eight a sudden banging and yelling would break out all through the base- ment; bells rang on all sides, blue-aproned men rushed through the passages, our service lifts came down with a simultaneous crash, and the waiters on all five floors began shouting Italian oaths down the 25 shafts. I don't remember all our duties, but they included making tea, coffee and chocolate, fetching meals from the kitchen, wines from the cellar and fruit and so forth from the dining-room, slicing bread, making toast, rolling pats of butter, measuring jam, opening milk- cans, counting lumps of sugar, boiling eggs, cooking porridge, pound- 30 ing ice, grinding coffee—all this for from a hundred to two hundred customers. The kitchen was thirty yards away, and the dining-room sixty or seventy yards. Everything we sent up in the service lifts had to be covered by a voucher, and the vouchers had to be carefully filed, and there was trouble if even a lump of sugar was lost. Besides this, we 35 had to supply the staff with bread and coffee, and fetch the meals for the waiters upstairs. All in all, it was a complicated job.

I calculated that one had to walk and run about fifteen miles during the day, and yet the strain of the work was more mental than physical. Nothing could be easier, on the face of it, than this stupid scullion 40 work, but it is astonishingly hard when one is in a hurry. One has to leap to and fro between a multitude of jobs—it is like sorting a pack of cards against the clock. You are, for example, making toast, when bang! down comes a service lift with an order for tea, rolls and three different kinds of jam, and simultaneously bang! down comes another 45 demanding scrambled eggs, coffee and grapefruit; you run to the kitchen for the eggs and to the dining-room for the fruit, going like lightning so as to be back before your toast burns, and having to remember about the tea and coffee, besides half a dozen other orders that are still pending; and at the same time some waiter is following 50 you and making trouble about a lost bottle of soda-water, and you are arguing with him. It needs more brains than one might think. Mario said, no doubt truly, that it took a year to make a reliable cafetier.

The time between eight and half-past ten was a sort of delirium. Sometimes we were going as though we had only five minutes to live; 55 sometimes there were sudden lulls when the orders stopped and everything seemed quiet for a moment. Then we swept up the litter from the floor, threw down fresh sawdust, and swallowed gallipots of wine or coffee or water—anything, so long as it was wet. Very often we used to break off chunks of ice and suck them while we worked. The 60 heat among the gas-fires was nauseating; we swallowed quarts of drink during the day, and after a few hours even our aprons were drenched with sweat. At times we were hopelessly behind with the work, and some of the customers would have gone without their breakfast, but Mario always pulled us through. He had worked fourteen years in the 65 cafeterie, and he had the skill that never wastes a second between jobs. The Magyar was very stupid and I was inexperienced, and Boris was inclined to shirk, partly because of his lame leg, partly because he was ashamed of working in the cafeterie after being a waiter; but Mario was wonderful. The way he would stretch his great arms right across 70 the cafeterie to fill a coffee-pot with one hand and boil an egg with the other, at the same time watching toast and shouting directions to the Magyar, and between whiles singing snatches from *Rigoletto*, was beyond all praise.

		Marks
(a)	Show how the first two sentences establish the difficult conditions in which the men work.	4
(b)	How does the description of the Magyar (lines 14-16) convey the writer's dislike of him?	2
(c)	Comment on THREE details in the description of the first *coup de feu* (lines 20-26) to illustrate the writer's apt choice of words.	3
(d)	How does the writer convey the demanding and confusing nature of the work? Refer to FOUR details or phrases to support the points you make.	8
(e)	Comment on the descriptions of Mario in order to bring out the writer's attitude towards him.	3
	Total	20

10. **Afternoons** by *Philip Larkin*

Summer is fading:
The leaves fall in ones and twos
From trees bordering
The new recreation ground.
In the hollows of afternoons   5
Young mothers assemble
At swing and sandpit
Setting free their children.

Behind them, at intervals,
Stand husbands in skilled trades,   10
An estateful of washing,
And the albums, lettered
Our Wedding, lying
Near the television:
Before them, the wind   15
Is ruining their courting-places

That are still courting-places
(But the lovers are all in school),
And their children, so intent on
Finding more unripe acorns,   20
Expect to be taken home.
Their beauty has thickened.
Something is pushing them
To the side of their own lives.

		Marks

(a)   What, if anything, is the significance of the title of the poem?   2

(b)   The poem could not have been written before the middle of this century. What evidence is there for this fact in the poem itself?   2

(c)   What impressions do you get of the lives of the young mothers described in the poem?   4

(d)   Do you think the poet feels any sympathy for the young mothers?   2

(e)   Explain carefully the meaning of *And their children, so intent on/Finding more unripe acorns,/Expect to be taken home* (lines 19-21). What is suggested about the character of the children in these lines?   2

(f)   Explain and bring out the effectiveness of each of the following images:
    (i)   *the hollows of afternoons* (line 5)
    (ii)   *An estateful of washing* (line 11)
    (iii)   *Something is pushing them/To the side of their own lives* (lines 23-24)   6

(g)   Would you recommend this poem to a friend? Give brief reasons.   2

Total   20

11.   *From* **Oliver Twist** *by Charles Dickens (adapted)*

Near to that part of the Thames on which the church at Rotherhithe
abuts, where the buildings on the banks are dirtiest and the vessels on
the river blackest with the dust of colliers and the smoke of close-built
low-roofed houses, there exists the filthiest, the strangest, the most
extraordinary of the many localities that are hidden in London, wholly 5
unknown, even by name, to the great mass of its inhabitants.

In such a neighbourhood, the warehouses are roofless and empty; the walls are crumbling down; the windows are windows no more; the doors are falling into the streets; the chimneys are blackened, but they yield no smoke. Thirty or forty years ago, before losses and chancery 10 suits came upon it, it was a thriving place; but now it is a desolate island indeed. The houses have no owners; they are broken open, and entered upon by those who have the courage; and there they live, and there they die.

In an upper room of one of these houses—a detached house of fair size, 15 ruinous in other respects, but strongly defended at door and window—there were assembled three men, who, regarding each other every now and then with looks expressive of perplexity and expectation, sat for some time in profound and gloomy silence.

It being now dark, the shutter was closed, and a candle lighted and 20 placed upon the table. The terrible events of the last two days had made a deep impression on all three, increased by the danger and uncertainty of their own position. They drew their chairs closer together, starting at every sound. They spoke little, and that in whispers, and were as silent and awe-stricken as if the remains of the 25 murdered woman lay in the next room.

They had sat thus, some time, when suddenly was heard a hurried knocking at the door below.

Crackit went to the window, and shaking all over, drew in his head. There was no need to tell them who it was; his pale face was enough. 30

"We must let him in," he said, taking up the candle.

"Isn't there any help for it?" asked the other man in a hoarse voice.

"None. He *must* come in."

Crackit went down to the door, and returned followed by a man with the lower part of his face buried in a handkerchief, and another tied 35 over his head under his hat. He drew them slowly off. Blanched face, sunken eyes, hollow cheeks, beard of three days' growth, wasted flesh, short thick breath; it was the very ghost of Sikes.

"Damn you all!" said Sikes, passing his hand across his forehead. "Have you nothing to say to me?"   40

There was an uneasy movement among them, but nobody spoke.

"You that keep this house," said Sikes, turning his face to Crackit, "do you mean to sell me, or to let me lie here till this hunt is over?"

"You may stop here, if you think it safe," returned the person addressed, after some hesitation.   45

113

There were lights gleaming below, voices in loud and earnest conversation, the tramp of hurried footsteps—endless they seemed in
number—crossing the nearest wooden bridge. One man on horseback
seemed to be among the crowd; for there was the noise of hoofs
rattling on the uneven pavement. The gleam of lights increased; the 50
footsteps came more thickly and noisily on. Then came a loud knocking at the door, and then a hoarse murmur from such a multitude of
angry voices as would have made the boldest quail.

"Help!" shrieked the boy in a voice that rent the air. "He's here!
Break down the door!"   55

"In the King's name," cried voices without; and the hoarse cry arose
again, but louder. Strokes, thick and heavy, rattled upon the door and
lower window-shutters.

"Damn you!" cried the desperate ruffian, throwing up the sash and
menacing the crowd. "Do your worst! I'll cheat you yet!"   60

Of all the terrific yells that ever fell on mortal ears, none could exceed
the cry of the infuriated throng. Some shouted to those who were
nearest to set the house on fire; others roared to the officers to shoot
him dead. Among them all, none showed such fury as the man on
horseback, who, throwing himself out of the saddle, and bursting 65
through the crowd as if he were parting water, cried, beneath the
window, in a voice that rose above all others, "Twenty guineas to the
man who brings a ladder!"

The nearest voices took up the cry, and hundreds echoed it. Some
called for ladders, some for sledge-hammers; some ran with torches to 70
and fro as if to seek them, and still came back and roared again; some
spent their breath on impotent curses and execrations; some pressed
forward with the ecstasy of madmen, and thus impeded the progress
of those below; some among the boldest attempted to climb up by the
water-spout and crevices in the wall; and all waved to and fro, in the 75
darkness beneath, like a field of corn moved by an angry wind, and
joined from time to time in one loud furious roar.

"The tide," cried the murderer, as he staggered back into the room,
and shut the faces out, "the tide was in as I came up. Give me a rope, a
long rope. They're all in front. I may drop into the Folly Ditch, and 80
clear off that way. Give me a rope, or I shall do three more murders
and kill myself."

Marks

(a) How do the first two paragraphs (lines 1-14) establish an air of squalor
     and decay?   6

(b) In what ways does the writer convey the evil and power of the murderer
     Sikes?   4

(c) Comment on the various sounds described in lines 46-58, showing what
     they contribute to the developing situation.   4

(d) Show how a sense of wildness and excitement is generated in the storm-
     ing of the house (lines 61-77).   6

                                                              Total   20

12. **In Oak Terrace** *by Tony Connor*

Old and alone, she sits at nights,
nodding before the television.
The house is quiet now. She knits,
rises to put the kettle on,

watches a cowboy's killing, reads   5
the local Births and Deaths, and falls
asleep at "Growing stock-piles of war-heads".
A world that threatens worse ills

fades. She dreams of a life spent
in the one house: suffers again   10
poverty, sickness, abandonment,
a child's death, a brother's brain

melting to madness. Seventy years
of common trouble; the kettle sings.
At midnight she says her silly prayers,   15
and takes her teeth out, and collects her night-things.

                                                              Marks
(a) What impressions of the old woman do you get from the poem?   5

(b) How do the things she sees on television or reads in the newspapers
     contrast with or reflect her own sufferings?   4

(c) What effects are created by each of the following?
     (i)   *The house is quiet now* (line 3)
     (ii)   *melting* (line 13)
     (iii) *Seventy years/of common trouble* (lines 13-14)
     (iv)   *sings* (line 14)   6

(d) What do the observations of the woman's actions in the last two lines of
     the poem suggest are the poet's feelings about her?   4

(e) Comment on the poet's use of rhyme.   1
                                                              Total   20

13. *From* **Mr Stone and the Knights Companion** *by V. S. Naipaul*

The day before they left the skies cleared and in the afternoon they went for a walk. Their way led along cliffs which, rimmed with deep white footpaths, fell to the sea in partial ruin. It was still cold, and they encountered no more than half a dozen people on the way. Just when they were getting tired and craving for sweet things, they saw a neat 5 sign promising tea fifty yards on.

The establishment was as neat as the sign. A clean white card on each crisp checked tablecloth, a blue cloth alternating with a red, announced the owner as Miss Chichester. Miss Chichester was what her name, her establishment and her card promised. She was middle- 10 aged, stout, with a large bosom. Her brisk manner proclaimed the dignity of labour as a discovery she expected to be universally shared; her accent was genteel without exaggeration; in her dress and discreet make-up there was the hint, that though perhaps widowed and in straitened circumstances, she was not letting herself go.   15

Only one of the tables was occupied, by a party of three, a man and two women. The women were as stout as Miss Chichester, but an overflow of flesh here and there, a coarseness in legs, complexion and hair, in coats, hats and shiny new bags suggested only a cosy grossness, as well as the fixed stares through spectacles in ill-chosen frames, and the 20 smooth swollen hands firmly grasping bags on thighs whose fatness was accentuated by the opened coats, lower buttons alone undone. The man was a wizened creature with narrow, sloping shoulders loose within a stiff new tweed jacket, his thin hair, the flex of his hearing-aid and the steel rims of his spectacles contributing to a general impres- 25 sion of perilous attenuation, as did the hand-rolled cigarette which, thin and wrinkled like the neck of the smoker, lay dead and forgotten between thin lips. He showed no interest in the arrival of Margaret and Mr Stone, and continued to stare at the checked tablecloth, sitting between the two women (one his wife, the other—what?) who looked 30 like his keepers.

Their silence imposed silence on Margaret and Mr Stone as well, and even when Miss Chichester brought out tea for the party the silence continued. The man fell wordlessly on plates and pots and tasteful jugs as though he had been sparing his energies for this moment. He 35 attacked the dainty sandwiches, the fresh scones, the home-made jam; and with every mouthful he appeared to grow more energetic, restless and enterprising. His thin, hairy hand shot out in all directions, making to grab teapots, cake-plates, jam-bowls, gestures so decisive and of such authority that his keepers who were at first inclined to 40 deflect his pouncing actions, surrendered entirely, and contented themselves with salvaging what food they could. Abruptly the eater finished. He worked his lips over his teeth, made a few sucking noises, and perceptibly the expression of blind eagerness gave way to the earlier sour dejection. He stared straight ahead, at nothing; while his 45 keepers, rescuing their tea interlude from premature extinction, intermittently nibbled at bread and butter as if without appetite. Throughout there had been no speech at the table.

The habit of examining people older than himself was one into which Mr Stone had been falling during the past year. It was something he 50 fought against; observation told him that only women, very young children and very old men inspected and assessed others of their group with such intensity. But now in spite of himself he stared with horror and fascination, and found that, as the eater's actions had grown more frenzied, his own had grown exaggeratedly slow. 55

Their own tea arrived and they prepared to begin. Attempting to break the silence Mr Stone found that he whispered, and the whisper was like gunshot. Silence continued, except for the kitchen clatter and the thumps of Miss Chichester's shoes.

And then silence vanished. The door was pushed vigorously open and 60 there entered a very tall man and a very small fair girl. The man was in mountaineering clothes, like one equipped for a Himalayan or at least Alpine expedition. He carried rucksack and ropes; his thick rough trousers were tucked into thick woollen socks, and these disappeared into massive lustreless boots with extraordinarily thick soles. He 65 created, by his masculine entry and the laying down of detachable burdens, as much noise as for two or three. The girl was soft and mute. Her slacks, imperfectly and tremulously filled, suggested only fragility; so did her light-blue silk scarf. The pale colours of her clothes, the milky fawn of her raincoat, and the style of her pale tan shoes marked 70 her as a European.

Sitting at the table, his rough-trousered knees reaching to the table-cloth, dwarfing the table and the flower vase, the mountaineer extended a greeting, accompanied by a bow, to the room. His English was only slightly accented. 75

The eater and his keepers nodded. Mr Stone's eyebrows dropped, like one surprised and affronted. Margaret was only momentarily distracted from scones and jam.

But the man filled the room. His speech created a conversational momentum on its own; the silence of others did not matter. He said 80 that he was Dutch; that in his country there were no mountains; that Cornwall was indescribably picturesque. All this in English which, because he was Dutch, was perfect; and the linguistic performance was made more impressive by his occasional sentences in Dutch to his mute scarfed companion. 85

He required no replies, but the eater and his keepers were steadily drawn into his talk. From nods and exclamations of "Yes" and "Oh!" they went on the speak approvingly of his English. These remarks the Dutchman translated to his companion, who, raising embarrassed eyes, appeared to receive the compliments as her own. 90

(a) By commenting on THREE details in the description of the two women (lines 17-22), show that the writer's view of them is unfavourable. 6

(b) What is the writer expressing by the question within brackets in line 30? 1

(c) Bring out the effectiveness of the continued reference to *the eater and his keepers*. 2

(d) Comment on the description of the eater's actions (lines 34-48) in order to bring out the *horror and fascination* which Mr Stone feels, and which the the reader is expected to feel, at witnessing these happenings. 5

(e) What impressions do you get of (i) Miss Chichester, (ii) the Dutchman? 6

Total 20

14. Coalmine *by Margaret Stanley-Wrench*

A coalmine is an etching the steel bites
Deep on a pewter sky. Over the pit
A black sun turns, the wheel a skeleton
Helios, and girders, ladders, struts
Weave coarse black lace of iron over the sky. 5
Like men in trains, insular, apathetic
The rows of houses staring face to face
Reflect the whey-blue sky in their bleak windows.
Slag heaps point like the conical Tuscan hills.

And a whippet, yellow as a wireworm, races through the 10
   clinkers.
Flat as the tang of tarnished metal, the smell
Of the mine clings here, the tide of it, in blackness
Flows over the country. Yet calm as the teams that pull
Great waggons, scarlet and blue, heaped high with corn,
Pit ponies graze and blink, their felted flanks 15
Dusty with the thin, strained yellow light.
But, as the dark halo of suffering marks out
Those whom time and pain have worn away,
These patient beasts, grazing the blackened grass
Have darkness still around them, and the smell 20
Of the mine like death to haunt the tainted field.

Marks

(a) What do the images in lines 1-5 suggest are the poet's feelings about the coalmine? 5

(b) Explain exactly what is meant by *the dark halo of suffering marks out/Those whom time and pain have worn away* (lines 17-18). 2

(c) Comment on the comparison of the houses to men in trains in the first stanza. 2

(d)   Bring out the effectiveness of each of the following:
      (i)   *like the conical Tuscan hills* (line 9)
      (ii)   *the tide of it, in blackness/Flows over the country* (lines 12-13)
      (iii) *graze and blink* (line 15)
      (iv)   *the tainted field* (line 21)   8

(e)   Examine the poet's use of colour in the poem.   3

                                                          Total   20

15.   *From* **The Devils** *by John Whiting (adapted)*

CAST
GRANDIER   a priest of Loudun in France in the seventeenth century.
He has been found guilty of sorcery, or dealings with the devil, but
although he has several sins upon his conscience he is not guilty of this
one.

LAUBARDEMONT   the King's Special Commissioner, in charge of the
trial and carrying out of the sentence on GRANDIER.

D'ARMAGNAC⎱   important Officials of Loudun.
  DE CERISAY⎰

SCENE
A public place.
A large crowd. Town and country people. Yawning, at ease, calling to
each other. Apart: an enclosure holding some well-dressed women of the
bougeoisie. Chatter from them. There is a CLERK *within a mountain of*
books.

Sudden silence. The CLERK *rises. He reads:*

CLERK: Urbain Grandier, you have been found guilty of commerce
with the devil. It is ordered that you be taken to the Place Sainte-
Croix, tied to a stake, and burned alive: after which your ashes will be
scattered to the four winds. Lastly, before sentence is carried out you
will be subjected to the Question, both ordinary and extraordinary. 5
Pronounced at Loudun, 18 August 1634, and executed the same day.

GRANDIER: My lords, I call God to witness that I have never been a
sorcerer. The only magic I have practised is that of the Holy Scripture.
I am innocent.

Silence. Then murmurs from the women: a silly laugh.   10

I am innocent, and I am afraid. I fear for my salvation. I am prepared
to go and meet God, but the horrible torment you have ordered for me
on the way may drive my wretched soul to despair. Despair, my lords.
It is the gravest of sins. It is the short way to eternal damnation. Surely
in your wisdom you do not mean to kill a soul. So may I ask you, in 15
your mercy, to mitigate, if only a little, my punishment.

GRANDIER *looks from face to face: silence.*

Very well. When I was a child I was told about the martyrs. I loved the men and women who died for the honour of Jesus Christ. In a time of loneliness I have often wished to be of their company. Now, foolish 20 and obscure priest that I am, I cannot presume to place myself among these great and holy men. But may I say that I have the hope in my heart that as this day ends Almighty God, my beloved Father in Heaven, will glance aside and let my suffering atone for my vain and disordered life. Amen. 25

Silence. Then somewhere in the crowd a man's voice clearly echoes GRAN-DIER's *amen. Then another. Silence again. Only the sound of a woman bitterly weeping.*

LAUBARDEMONT *to the Captain of the Guard:* Get them all out of here!

At once the guards begin to clear the place. The public go away along 30 *corridors and down steps, complaining, some protesting.* GRANDIER *is left with* LAUBARDEMONT, *the* CLERK, *and the judges.* DE CERISAY *and* D'ARMAGNAC *can be seen. They are apart, overlooking the scene.* LAUBARDEMONT *speaks to* GRANDIER:

LAUBARDEMONT: Confess your guilt. Tell us the names of your 35 accomplices. Then perhaps my lords, the judges, will consider your appeal.

GRANDIER: I cannot name accomplices I've never had, nor confess to crimes I've not done.

LAUBARDEMONT: This attitude will do you no good. You will suffer 40 for it.

GRANDIER: I know that. And I am proud.

LAUBARDEMONT: Proud sir? That word does not become your situation. Now look here, my dear fellow—untie his hands—this document is a simple confession. Here is a pen. Just put your name to this 45 paper and we can forget the next stage of the proceedings.

GRANDIER: You must excuse me. No.

LAUBARDEMONT: I just want your signature. Here. That's all.

GRANDIER: My conscience forbids me to put my name to something which is untrue. 50

LAUBARDEMONT: You'll save us all a lot of trouble if you'll sign. The document being true, of course. *He shouts:* True! You've been found guilty.

120

GRANDIER: I'm sorry.

LAUBARDEMONT: I fear for you, Grandier. I fear for you very much. 55
I have seen men before you take this brave stand in the shadow of the
Question.* It was unwise, Grandier. Think again.

GRANDIER: No.

LAUBARDEMONT: You will go into the darkness before your death.
Let me talk to you for a moment about pain. It is very difficult for us 60
standing here, both healthy men, to imagine the shattering effect of
agony. The sun's warm on your face at the moment, isn't it? And you
can curl your toes if you want in your slippers. You are alive, and you
know it. But when you are stretched out in that little room, with the
pain screaming through you like a voice, let me tell you what you will 65
think. First: how can man do this to man? Then: how can God allow
it? Then: there can be no God. Then: there is no God. The voice of
pain will grow stronger, and your resolution weaker. Despair, Grandier. You used the word yourself. You called it the gravest sin. Don't
reject God at this moment. Reconcile yourself. For you have bitterly 70
offended Him. Confess.

GRANDIER: No.

D'ARMAGNAC: Are those tears on Laubardemont's face?

DE CERISAY: I'm afraid so.

D'ARMAGNAC: Does he believe what he's saying? 75

DE CERISAY: Yes. Touching, isn't it?

LAUBARDEMONT to GRANDIER: Very well. I ask you once more.
Once more. Will you sign?

GRANDIER shakes his head.

LAUBARDEMONT: Take him away. 80

The guards surround GRANDIER and take him out.

*The Question is questioning under torture with a view to obtaining a
confession.

Marks

(a) What different methods does Laubardemont use to try to obtain a
confession from Grandier? 6

(b) Explain carefully the dramatic effects created, in their contexts, by each
of the following:

121

(i) the sudden silence as the Clerk rises
(ii) the Clerk's announcement (lines 1-6)
(iii) a silly laugh (line 10)
(iv) a man's voice echoing amen and a woman bitterly weeping (lines 26-28)
(v) Laubardemont's command (line 29)   10

(c) What does Grandier's speech (lines 7-25) reveal of his state of mind and character?   3

(d) What is De Cerisay expressing by the remark, *Yes. Touching, isn't it* (line 76)?   1

Total   20

16. **First Child** *by Vernon Scannell*
(For John and Jean Bourne)

What fed their apprehension was the fears
Of loud compulsory insomnia,
Their little liberties abruptly cancelled,
The marvel of their marriage darkening
Beneath a wagging, sanitary bunting: 5
All these intrusions they would have to face.
But when the niggling interdicts and chill
Labours took up threatened residence
These seemed to be quite friendly after all.

What they had not prepared themselves to meet   10
Was this: the soft catastrophes, the sly
Menaces whose names are hard to spell
Creeping to her cot, the quiet killers
Loading their white guns and brooding over
That innocent and O, so fragile head.   15

Marks

(a) What, according to the poet, are the couple's thoughts and feelings about the future birth of their first child?   4

(b) How does the second verse extend the range of thought of the first verse?   2

(c) Explain carefully the meaning of the following phrases:
     (i) *niggling interdicts* (line 7)
     (ii) *threatened residence (line 8)*
     (iii) *whose names are hard to spell* (line 12)   6

(d) Show how an impression of stealth and hostility is conveyed by the images of the second verse.   6

(e) What emotions are aroused about the baby by the last line of the poem?   2

Total   20

122

17.   *From* **Over the Bridge** *by Richard Church*

So I found myself in the boys' school, and there I endured its pro-
cessing until I was twelve, when we left Battersea. My brother's career
was the model on which I was expected to shape my own. Unhappily
for me, the school had a system by which a master went up with his
class of boys, standard by standard, from the first to the seventh, the 5
ex-seventh being run by the deputy-Head, a gentle, bearded scholar
who walked alone. It was he who finally took my brother under his
wing, and made him win a scholarship to the secondary school
attached to Battersea Polytechnic. Fifty years ago such scholarships
were rare. All through these school years Jack's health was faultless. 10
He never had to stay away from school, or avoid doing his homework,
on which he spent a couple of hours every evening, after a day at
school that lasted from 8.40 a.m. until 5 p.m., with a midday break
from 12 until 1.40.

The lower standards up to the 5th finished at 4.30. Otherwise, the 15
boys had to work just as hard. I found it heavy going, especially as the
emphasis was on arithmetic. The arts were not encouraged at Surrey
Lane, perhaps because it was a higher-grade school, though to what
that aspiration pointed I did not discover.

The system of the master remaining with his class for several years, 20
from standards one to seven, which meant practically the whole six
years of a boy's life in the school, was unfortunate for me because I had
the master who had formerly led my brother through the same groves.
His name was Mr Meek, and he was trusted by my parents because he
had always been so helpful and favourable to Jack, a brilliant pupil. 25
There was some professional fellow-feeling, too, between him and
Mother. Thus he received me with marked interest and was prepared
to further my education, as he had furthered my brother's, with some
particularity and enthusiasm.

Perhaps the fact that I was a precocious reader gave him false hopes. 30
He may have expected that I should bring the same precocity into my
dealings with vulgar fractions and the decimal system, and, later with
mensuration, the elements of Euclid and the measurement of water
flowing in and out of tanks, simultaneously, through pipes of differing
diameters.   35

He was quickly discomfited. He soon found that I had no aptitude for
figures because I was not rational in my way of life. He also found that
I was an apprehensive boy, groping my way through the world as a
snail does, by the aid of instinctive horns that retracted with lightning
speed before the least opposition. Mr Meek evidently disliked snails, 40
and before long he began to treat me like one. This tended to make me
keep my horns permanently withdrawn, while I was in school and
subject to his increasingly chilly criticism.

(a)   What is the writer's attitude towards (i) the Surrey Lane School, (ii) his
      brother Jack?   4

(b)   What impressions of Mr Meek do you derive from this passage?   4

(c)   Explain carefully the meaning of:
      (i)   *endured its processing* (lines 1-2)
      (ii) *led my brother through the same groves* (line 23)
      (iii) *some professional fellow-feeling* (line 26)   6

(d)   Comment on the effectiveness of the way the writer makes the point
      (in lines 30-35) that he *had no aptitude for figures*.   3

(e)   Comment on the comparison of the boy to a snail (lines 37-43) in order to
      bring out how effectively the writer conveys the boy's state of mind and
      Mr Meek's attitude towards him.   3

                                                          Total   20

18.   **Thistles** by *Ted Hughes*

Against the rubber tongues of cows and the hoeing
   hands of men
Thistles spike the summer air
Or crackle open under a blue-black pressure.

Every one a revengeful burst
Of resurrection, a grasped fistful   5
Of splintered weapons and Icelandic frost thrust up

From the underground stain of a decayed Viking.
They are like pale hair and the gutturals of dialects.
Every one manages a plume of blood.

Then they grow grey, like men.   10
Mown down, it is a feud. Their sons appear,
Stiff with weapons, fighting back over the same ground.

(a)   Show how the images in lines 4-7 and in lines 11-12 convey the violent
      nature of the thistles.   8

(b)   Explain the meaning and bring out the effectiveness of each of the follow-
      ing images:
      (i)   *rubber tongues of cows* (line 1)
      (ii) *spike the summer air* (line 2)
      (iii) *like pale hair and the gutturals of dialects* (line 8)
      (iv) *a plume of blood* (line 9)
      (v)   *Then they grow grey, like men* (line 10)   10

(c)   Would you recommend this poem to a friend? Give brief reasons.   2

                                                          Total   20

19. *From* **Odour of Chrysanthemums** *by D. H. Lawrence*

The house was quiet. Elizabeth Bates took off her hat and shawl, and
sat down. It was a few minutes past nine. She was startled by the rapid
chuff of the winding-engine at the pit, and the sharp whirr of the
brakes on the rope as it descended. She put her hand to her side,
saying aloud: "Good gracious!—it's only the nine o'clock deputy 5
going down," rebuking herself.

She sat still, listening. Half an hour of this, and she was wearied out.

"What am I working myself up like this for?" she said pitiably to
herself. "I s'll only be doing myself some damage."

She took out her sewing again.   10

At a quarter to ten there were footsteps. One person! She watched for
the door to open. It was an elderly woman, in a black bonnet and a
black woollen shawl—his mother. She was about sixty years old, pale,
with blue eyes, and her face all wrinkled and lamentable. She shut the
door and turned to her daughter-in-law peevishly.   15

"Eh, Lizzie, whatever shall we do, whatever shall we do!" she cried.

Elizabeth drew back a little, sharply.

"What is it, mother?" she said.

The elder woman seated herself on the sofa.

"I don't know, child, I can't tell you!"—she shook her head slowly. 20
Elizabeth sat watching her, anxious and vexed.

"I don't know," replied the grandmother, sighing very deeply.
"There's no end to my troubles, there isn't. The things I've gone
through, 'm sure it's enough—!" She wept without wiping her eyes,
the tears running.   25

"But, mother," interrupted Elizabeth, "what do you mean? What is
it?"

The grandmother slowly wiped her eyes. The fountains of her tears
were stopped by Elizabeth's directness. She wiped her eyes slowly.

"Poor child! Eh, you poor thing!" she moaned. "I don't know what 30
we're going to do, I don't—and you as you are—it's a thing, it is
indeed!"

Elizabeth waited.

"Is he dead?" she asked, and at the words her heart swung violently, though she felt a slight flush of shame at the ultimate extravagance of 35 the question. Her words sufficiently frightened the old lady, brought her to herself.

"Don't say so, Elizabeth! We'll hope it's not as bad as that; no, may the Lord spare us that, Elizabeth. Jack Rigley came just as I was sittin' down to a glass afore going to bed, an' 'e said: ' 'Appen you'll go down 40 th' line, Mrs Bates. Walt's had an accident. 'Appen you'll go an' sit wi' 'er till we can get him home.' I hadn't time to ask him a word afore he was gone. An' I put my bonnet on an' come straight down, Lizzie. I thought to myself: 'Eh, that poor blessed child, if anybody should come an' tell her of a sudden, there's no knowin' what'll 'appen to 'er.' 45 You mustn't let it upset you, Lizzie."

Elizabeth's thoughts were busy elsewhere. If he was killed—would she be able to manage on the little pension and what she could earn?—she counted up rapidly. If he was hurt—they wouldn't take him to the hospital—how tiresome he would be to nurse!—but 50 perhaps she'd be able to get him away from the drink and his hateful ways. She would—while he was ill. The tears offered to come to her eyes at the picture. But what sentimental luxury was this she was beginning? She turned to consider the children. At any rate she was absolutely necessary for them. They were her business. 55

"Ay!" repeated the old woman, "it seems but a week or two since he brought me his first wages. Ay—he was a good lad, Elizabeth, he was, in his way. I don't know why he got to be such a trouble, I don't. He was a happy lad at home, only full of spirits. But there's no mistake he's been a handful of trouble, he has! I hope the Lord'll spare him to 60 mend his ways. I hope so. I hope so. You've had a sight o' trouble with him, Elizabeth, you have indeed. But he was a jolly enough lad wi' me, he was, I can assure you. I don't know how it is . . ."

The old woman continued to muse aloud, a monotonous irritating sound, while Elizabeth thought concentratedly, startled once, when 65 she heard the winding-engine chuff quickly, and the brakes skirr with a shriek. Then she heard the engine more slowly, and the brakes made no sound. The old woman did not notice. Elizabeth waited in suspense. The mother-in-law talked, with lapses into silence.

"But he wasn't your son, Lizzie, an' it makes a difference. Whatever 70 he was, I remember him when he was little, an' I learned to understand him and make allowances. You've got to make allowances for them—"

It was half-past ten, and the old woman was saying: "But it's trouble from beginning to end; you're never too old for trouble, never too old for that—" when the gate banged, and there were heavy feet on the steps.

"I'll go, Lizzie, let me go," cried the old woman, rising. But Elizabeth was at the door. It was a man in pit-clothes.

"They're bringin' 'im, Missis," he said. Elizabeth's heart halted a moment. Then it surged on again, almost suffocating her.

"Is he—is it bad?" she asked.

The man turned away, looking at the darkness:

"The doctor says 'e'd been dead hours. 'E saw 'im i' th' lamp-cabin."

The old woman, who stood just behind Elizabeth, dropped into a chair, and folded her hands, crying: "Oh, my boy, my boy!"

"Hush!" said Elizabeth, with a sharp twitch of a frown. "Be still, mother, don't waken th' children: I wouldn't have them down for anything!"

		Marks
(a)	What evidence is there in lines 1-12 to indicate that Elizabeth is worried about something?	3
(b)	Trace carefully Elizabeth's various responses to her mother-in-law, and the causes of her responses, in lines 16-37.	4
(c)	What impressions of the mother-in-law do you derive from (i) lines 22-25, (ii) lines 38-46?	3
(d)	What aspects of Elizabeth's character are shown in lines 47-55?	4
(e)	Comment on the mother-in-law's attitude to her son.	2
(f)	Show how the differing reactions of Elizabeth and her mother-in-law to the news of the man's death (lines 80-89) reveal wide differences in character and outlook.	3
(g)	Why does the miner turn away and look at the darkness (line 83)?	1
	Total	20

20. **Pet Shop** *by Louis MacNeice*

Cold blood or warm, crawling or fluttering
Bric-à-brac, all are here to be bought,
Noisy or silent, python or myna,
Fish with long silk trains like dowagers,
Monkeys lost to thought.   5

In a small tank tiny enamelled
Green terrapin jostle, in a cage a crowd
Of small birds elbow each other and bicker
While beyond the ferrets, eardrum, eyeball
Find that macaw too loud.   10

Here behind glass lies a miniature desert,
The sand littered with rumpled gauze
Discarded by snakes like used bandages;
In the next door desert fossilized lizards
Stand in a pose, a pause.   15

But most of the customers want something comfy—
Rabbit, hamster, potto, puss—
Something to hold on the lap and cuddle
Making believe it will return affection
Like some neutered succubus.   20

Purr then or chirp, you are here for our pleasure,
Here at the mercy of our whim and purse;
Once there was the wild, now tanks and cages,
But we can offer you a home, a haven,
That might prove even worse.   25

		Marks

(a)   Show how the poet suggests the crowded and varied life of the pet shop in the first fifteen lines of the poem.   7

(b)   What exactly is meant by the statement *eardrum, eyeball/Find that macaw too loud* (lines 9-10)?   1

(c)   What effects are created by each of the following?
    (i)   *all are here to be bought* (line 2)
    (ii) *long silk trains like dowagers* (line 4)
    (iii) *like used bandages* (line 13)   6

(d)   What, according to the poet, is the main reason why most customers buy their pets? What does the poet think of this attitude and how convincingly does he convey his opinion?   6

Total   20